Middle Level

Vocabulary Drills

Jamestown's Reading Improvement

Edward B. Fry, Ph.D.

a division of NTC/Contemporary Publishing Group
Lincolnwood, Illinois USA

Acknowledgments

Acknowledgment is gratefully made to the following publishers, authors, and agents for permission to reprint these works. Every effort has been made to determine copyright owners. In the case of any omissions, the Publishers will be pleased to make suitable acknowledgments in future editions.

"Laurel and Hardy: The Early Days," *Real World,* King Features Syndicate, Inc.

"Masters of Comedy," *Real World,* King Features Syndicate, Inc.

"Caring for a Cat" and "Cat Communication," excerpts from *The World Book Encyclopedia,* Vol. 3. © 1999 World Book, Inc. By permission of the publisher. http//www.worldbook.com

"In-Line Skating." Reprinted from *Extreme Sports Almanac* by Don Koeppel. © 1988 by Lowell House. Used with permission of NTC/Contemporary Publishing Group, Inc.

"Debris on Earth" by Nancy Day. Excerpted from *Odyssey*'s December 1991 issue: *Space Junk.* © 1991, Cobblestone Publishing Company, 30 Grove Street, Suite C, Peterborough, NH 03458. Reprinted by permission of the publisher.

"Light Pollution" by Terence Dickinson. Excerpted from "City Light vs. Starlight," in *Odyssey*'s December 1991 issue: *Space Junk.* © 1991, Cobblestone Publishing Company, 30 Grove Street, Suite C, Peterborough, NH 03458. Reprinted by permission of the publisher.

"Fresco Painting," excerpt from *The World Book Encyclopedia,* Vol. 7. © 1992 World Book, Inc. http//www.worldbook.com

"Oil Painting," excerpt from *The World Book Encyclopedia,* Vol. 15. © 1992 World Book, Inc. http//www.worldbook.com

"What is a Skeleton?" and "The Human Skeleton." Reprinted from *The Big Book of Bones* by Claire Llewellyn. © 1998 by Macdonald Young Books. Used with permission of Peter Bendrick Books.

Cover Design: Lightbourne

ISBN: 0-8092-0355-3
Published by Jamestown Publishers,
a division of NTC/Contemporary Publishing Group, Inc.,
4255 West Touhy Avenue,
Lincolnwood (Chicago), Illinois 60712-1975, U.S.A.

Manufactured in the United States of America.

3 4 5 6 7 8 9 10 021 0 1 9 8 7 6 5 4 3 2 1

Contents

To the Student

Introduction

Why build your vocabulary?

The aim of *Vocabulary Drills* is to help you learn how to approach new words and to become more comfortable with the language—free to explore new words and their meanings. In this book you will work with useful vocabulary that is presented in reading selections on many subjects and from many different types of sources. As you read the selections and do the exercises that accompany them, you will be developing your skills in dealing with new words—skills that you can carry over to your own reading.

Using Context

One of the most important skills you will learn is using context to get some idea of the meaning of an unfamiliar word. Context is the setting of the word—the ideas in the words and sentences that surround it. A word in a sentence carries an idea that fits in with the meaning of the whole sentence, and of the paragraph in which the sentence is located.

When you are reading on your own and come across an unfamiliar word, you don't usually want to stop reading to check the word in a dictionary. You should just try to get a fair sense of the word's meaning from its context and keep on reading. You can often come quite close to the meaning of a word by making a guess at it, based on the context. That is a skill you will develop in this book.

Learning About Roots

Another way people build their vocabularies is by learning about the roots of the language—the parts of English words that are based on other, older languages. Many English words are based on word parts borrowed from the ancient Latin and Greek languages. The Word Study lessons will help you learn the meanings of some Greek and Latin roots and of some words that contain those roots. You can then use your knowledge of roots to help you figure out the meanings of unfamiliar words that you meet in your own reading.

How to Use This Book

Vocabulary Drills is divided into 32 lessons. Every fifth lesson is a Review and Extension lesson that provides additional work with the words and word parts introduced in the four lessons preceding it.

The ideal way to approach the lessons and exercises is to work through the exercises on your own. Then, if possible, correct your answers in a group with classmates using the Answer Key provided by your teacher. Using words aloud and hearing them spoken helps to make them a part of your vocabulary. Talking about the words and discussing the answers to the exercises will help you better understand the words and how they are used.

Meeting Words in Context

Each of these odd-numbered lessons begins with a short reading passage that contains the vocabulary words you will work with in the lessons. The passages are taken from many kinds of reading material, including newspapers, magazines, general fiction and nonfiction, textbooks, and reference materials.

The five vocabulary words in each passage appear in boldface type. As you read a passage, try to figure out the meanings of the boldfaced words from the way they are used. Pay close attention to the ideas contained in the words and sentences that surround each vocabulary word. Try to understand how the vocabulary word fits in with those ideas.

The reading passage is followed by a Personal Words section. Here you write two words from the passage—*not* the boldfaced words—whose meanings you are not sure of. Make a guess at the meaning of each word, and write that meaning beside the word. Then at the end of the lesson, in the Personal Words Follow-up, compare your definition with a dictionary. Check to see how close your definition came to the one given in the dictionary. Finally, enter your two words and their correct definitions on the Personal Words pages that begin on page 124.

Four exercises follow each reading passage. In these exercises you will explore the meanings of the five vocabulary words as they are used in the passage. This is an important point for, as you know, many words have more than one meaning. There are many different exercise types, including multiple-choice, matching, sentence completion, word substitutions, and fill-in-the-blanks.

The exercises called Using Context ask you to try to figure out the meanings of the words from the way they are used in the passage. In Making Connections you match the words with synonyms and antonyms, match the words with their definitions, use the words in sentences, or complete analogies.

Word Study

In each of these even-numbered lessons an introduction teaches several Latin and Greek roots and other word parts. Following are three exercises in which you work with the roots and words parts that were introduced: a matching exercise; a true-false exercise; and a third exercise that may contain open-ended questions, fill-in-the-blanks, or a series of multiple-choice questions.

Review and Extension

The five exercises in this section build on your understanding of the words you have worked with in the preceding lessons.

Checking Your Work

Personal Words on pages 124–128 are your own new vocabulary words. Once you have recorded words and their definitions on these pages, read them over from time to time to make them part of you everyday writing and communicating.

The Glossary on pages 129–137 contains definitions of all the vocabulary words. Some exercises require the use of the glossary, others suggest that you use it if you cannot recall what a word means. Be sure when you consult the glossary that if more than one definition is given for a word you choose the one that has the meaning you are looking for.

Answer Key. Check your work by using the answer key provided by your teacher. Try to figure out why the correct answer was correct. If you are confused by an answer, discuss it with the other members of the group or with your teacher. Remember, your main goal is to develop your ability to learn and use words.

Word List. The Alphabetical Word and Word Part List on pages 138–140 is a handy reference that tells you which lesson introduced each vocabulary word.

Remember that the more words you know, the better you will understand what you read and the better you will be able to communicate. Good luck!

1 Laurel and Hardy: The Early Days

Laurel and Hardy both started out early in show business, thousands of miles apart. Born in 1890 in England, Laurel, whose real name was Arthur Stanley Jefferson, managed a little theater in his own attic when he was only nine. Oliver Norvell Hardy, born in Georgia in 1892, left home at the age of eight to travel with a **troupe** called Coburn's Minstrels.

By the time they were teenagers, beanpole Stan and butterball Ollie (who already weighed 250 pounds) had discovered that they could make people laugh. Both of them decided to pursue show business careers in earnest. Neither realized that he'd eventually **attain** fame only as part of a team.

Laurel came to the United States as an **understudy** to the great comedian Charlie Chaplin. After their show **folded,** Stan continued in vaudeville, the live variety entertainment of the day, with various partners.

Hardy began his film career in 1913, and Laurel began his in 1917. In those silent-movie days, a producer named Hal Roach was the king of comedy, working with popular comedians of the era. It was he who teamed Laurel and Hardy in 1927. They had already appeared in Hal Roach films together, but not as a team.

Both were **seasoned** performers, but neither was a big star. Laurel was then 37 years old. Hardy was 35.

Movies were filmed "off the cuff" then—almost made up as shooting went along. Laurel was especially good at inventing slapstick action. It was he who suggested that *The Battle of the Century,* one of Laurel and Hardy's funniest films, feature more pie-throwing than ever. At least 2,000 pies were flung in one long, crazy scene.

Personal Words

Choose two words from the selection that are unfamiliar to you or whose meanings you are not completely sure of. (Do not choose words that appear in boldfaced type.) Write the words on the lines provided. Beside each word write what you think it means, based on how it was used in the selection.

1. ____________________ : ____

____

2. ____________________ : ____

____

Using Context

Put an **X** in the box beside each correct answer. For clues to the meanings of words, reread the parts of the passage in which they appear.

1. From the name of the troupe Hardy traveled with as a child, you can tell that **troupe** means
   - ☐ a. a motorcycle gang.
   - ☐ b. boy scouts.
   - ☐ c. a group of performers.
   - ☐ d. a big, fancy car.

2. To **attain** fame means to
   - ☐ a. wish to be famous.
   - ☐ b. seek fame without success.
   - ☐ c. think little of fame.
   - ☐ d. succeed in becoming famous.

3. The sentence in which **folded** appears might have been written: Stan continued in vaudeville after Chaplin's show
   - ☐ a. closed.
   - ☐ b. returned.
   - ☐ c. went overseas.
   - ☐ d. got better.

4. From what is told of the careers of Laurel and Hardy before the word *seasoned* appears, you can guess that a **seasoned** performer is one who
   - ☐ a. performs only during a certain season.
   - ☐ b. takes only certain kinds of roles.
   - ☐ c. has become a big star.
   - ☐ d. has gained experience over time.

5. As **understudy** to Charlie Chaplin, Laurel
   - ☐ a. filled in for Chaplin if he couldn't perform.
   - ☐ b. carried Chaplin's makeup and costumes.
   - ☐ c. studied with Chaplin.
   - ☐ d. had the dressing room directly under Chaplin's.

Making Connections

A For each boldfaced vocabulary word in the following sentences choose a synonym and an antonym from the list. Write the synonyms and antonyms in the blanks.

experienced	**substitute**	**gain**	**group**	**closed**
lose	**individual**	**untried**	**opened**	**competitor**

1. Hardy left home at the age of eight to travel with a **troupe** called Coburn's Minstrels.

   Synonym: ____________________ Antonym: ____________________

2. Neither realized that he'd eventually **attain** fame only as part of a team.

   Synonym: ____________________ Antonym: ____________________

3. Laurel came to the United States as **understudy** to the great comedian Charlie Chaplin.

   Synonym: ____________________ Antonym: ____________________

4. After their show **folded,** Stan continued in vaudeville with various partners.

 Synonym: ______________________ Antonym: ______________________

5. Both were **seasoned** performers, but neither was a big star.

 Synonym: ______________________ Antonym: ______________________

B Complete the following analogies by inserting one of the five vocabulary words in the blank at the end of each one. Remember that in an analogy the last two words or phrases must be related to each other in the same way that the first two are related. The colon in an analogy is read "is to," and the symbol :: is read "as."

troupe **attain** **understudy** **folded** **seasoned**

1. teacher : substitute : : actor : ______________________
2. retreated : advanced : : opened : ______________________
3. embrace : hold : : reach : ______________________
4. beginner : inexperienced : : veteran : ______________________
5. athlete : team : : performer : ______________________

C Complete each sentence with the correct vocabulary word.

troupe **attain** **understudy** **folded** **seasoned**

1. Greta worked to ______________________ the next level of expertise in karate.
2. It takes a ______________________ chef to whip up a complicated sauce.
3. Ricardo auditioned for a spot in his favorite dance ______________________ .
4. Our corner grocery store ______________________ after 23 years in business.
5. Esther was an ______________________ to the star of the play.

Personal Words Follow-up

Use a dictionary to find the definitions for the personal words you chose at the beginning of this lesson. If a word has more than one meaning, look for the meaning that defines the word as it is used in the selection. Then write the words and their dictionary definitions in the Personal Words pages at the back of the book.

2 Word Study

The word *prefix* means, literally, "the part of the word that is fixed before the root." *Pre-* means "before." It forms the beginning of many common English words. The word *precook* means "to partially or entirely cook before final cooking." A word that appears often in the news and history books is *prejudice.* It means "an unfavorable opinion formed before all the facts are known." When you precede someone in line, you are before them.

Let's look at *predict.* The root *dict* means "to say" or "to proclaim." To predict something is to tell in advance that it is going to happen. *Dict* is also the root of the word *diction,* which refers to a person's style of speaking or writing.

The prefix that has the opposite meaning of *pre-* is *post-* , which means "after" or "following." A *postscript* is any material added to a book or letter, and *postpone* means "to put off to a later time."

Word Part	Meaning	English Word
pre-	before	precook, prejudice
dict	to say; to proclaim	prediction, diction
post-	after; following	postscript

Finding Meanings

Write each word or word part below beside its meaning.

pre- **prejudice** **post-** **diction** **precede**

1. opinion formed before the facts are known ____________________
2. before ____________________
3. to go before ____________________
4. after ____________________
5. manner of expressing ideas in words ____________________

True or False

Write T if a statement is true or F if it is false.

________ 1. To precede someone is to go after him or her.

________ 2. You would take a posttest after completing a project.

________ 3. If you have good diction, you express ideas well in words.

________ 4. If you have formed a prejudice against someone, you have done so only after examining all the facts.

________ 5. A good prediction would be that computers will someday be invented.

Answering Questions

1. If you prepay for a mail-order purchase, do you pay when you send in the order or when the purchased item arrives? ________________________________

   ____

2. If you form an opinion by prejudging, you are likely to develop a ________________.
3. Considering the fact that the root *dict* means "to say," what do you think happens when a person dictates a letter into a tape recorder? __________________________

   ____

4. What does it mean to postpone a party?______________________________

   ____

5. A person who foretells the future, or says what is going to happen, does what?__________

   ____

3 Masters of Comedy

With their **distinctive** voices, Laurel and Hardy moved easily from silent movies into the "talkies." They remained popular through the Great Depression, which started in 1929 and lasted for about 10 years. Americans may have been down-and-out, but they still needed entertainment.

The team **graduated** from two-reel films to full-length features. In all, they appeared together in 77 shorts and 28 feature films. Students of film say their best work was done in the 1920s and 1930s.

For **decades** more, the public enjoyed the derby-hatted duo, who faced more **tribulations** in two reels than most of us face in a year.

Surprisingly, the critics of their day didn't regard Stan and Ollie as great artists. Today, however, the tearful Laurel and the tie-twirling Hardy are considered important contributors to film comedy.

"Well, here's another fine mess you've gotten me into, Stanley," Ollie would whine. You could analyze their art for hours, and many scholars have. But the main thing is to just sit back and enjoy them.

Offscreen, Laurel and Hardy had separate interests and separate lives. But each admired the comedic artistry of the other.

After their retirement from films, the two toured abroad. Europeans loved them. In the United States today, a Laurel and Hardy **cult** still carries the torch of admiration for the two master zanies. Oliver Hardy died in 1957, and Stan Laurel died in 1965.

Personal Words

Choose two words from the selection that are unfamiliar to you or whose meanings you are not completely sure of. (Do not choose words that appear in boldfaced type.) Write the words on the lines provided. Beside each word write what you think it means, based on how it was used in the selection.

1. ____________________ : ______________________________________

____

2. ____________________ : ______________________________________

____

Using Context

Put an **X** in the box beside the best definition for each boldfaced word. For clues to the meanings of words, reread the parts of the passage in which they appear.

1. With their **distinctive** voices, Laurel and Hardy moved easily from silent movies into the "talkies."
   - ☐ a. loud
   - ☐ b. unpleasant
   - ☐ c. ordinary
   - ☐ d. unusual

2. The team **graduated** from two-reel films to full-length features.
   - ☐ a. got diplomas
   - ☐ b. moved to a higher level
   - ☐ c. alternated between
   - ☐ d. slowly got used to

3. For **decades** more, the public enjoyed the derby-hatted duo, who faced more tribulations in two reels than most of us face in a year.
   - ☐ a. periods of ten years
   - ☐ b. hundreds of days
   - ☐ c. periods of twenty years
   - ☐ d. an unknown period of time

4. For decades more, the public enjoyed the derby-hatted duo, who faced more **tribulations** in two reels than most of us face in a year.
   - ☐ a. movie directors
   - ☐ b. voice teachers
   - ☐ c. difficulties
   - ☐ d. good times or fun

5. In the United States today, a Laurel and Hardy **cult** still carries the torch of admiration for the two master zanies.
   - ☐ a. fan
   - ☐ b. group of admirers
   - ☐ c. actor's magazine
   - ☐ d. memorial statue

Making Connections

A Write each word from the list below in front of its definition as it is used in the selection.

distinctive **graduated** **decade** **tribulation** **cult**

1. ____________________ great trouble or distress
2. ____________________ passed from one level to a higher one
3. ____________________ group showing great admiration
4. ____________________ period of ten years
5. ____________________ special; recognizably different

B On the line next to each word or phrase, write the vocabulary word that is related to it. The related word may be a synonym, an antonym, or a definition for the vocabulary word.

distinctive **graduated** **decade** **tribulations** **cult**

1. progressed ____________________
2. difficulties ____________________
3. ordinary ____________________
4. woes ____________________
5. opponents ____________________
6. ten years ____________________
7. good times ____________________
8. failed ____________________
9. group of followers ____________________
10. special ____________________

C Complete each sentence with the correct vocabulary word.

distinctive **graduated** **decade** **tribulations** **cult**

1. Greg could still remember the day he ____________________ from his tricycle to a 20-inch bicycle with training wheels.
2. The girls talked for hours about the ____________________ of their favorite soap-opera characters.
3. The candy store had a ____________________ aroma of chocolate, licorice, and newsprint, all mixed together.
4. Years after his death, there is still a large ____________________ interested in the music and style of Elvis Presley.
5. Nora spent a lot of time daydreaming about exciting events she hoped would take place in her life over the next ____________________

Personal Words Follow-up

Use a dictionary to find the definitions for the personal words you chose at the beginning of this lesson. If a word has more than one meaning, look for the meaning that defines the word as it is used in the selection. Then write the words and their dictionary definitions in the Personal Words pages at the back of the book. How close did you come to figuring out their meanings for yourself?

4 Word Study

The prefix *com-* means "with," "together," or "thoroughly." The word *combine* means "to bring two or more things together to form something new." The two chemical elements hydrogen and oxygen combine to form water. *Compose* means "to put together." A story is composed by combining ideas, and a composer is someone who combines notes to make music. The result of composing is a composition. The Latin root *plere* means "to fill." The word *complete* means "finished," "whole," or "full."

The word *comfort* includes the root *fort,* which means "strong." To offer comfort is to bring someone strength and hope. In music the word *forte* means "in a loud or forceful manner." This notation on a piece of music means the passage is to be played loudly.

The prefix *con-* can also be combined with many word parts or roots to add the meaning "together" or "with." If you are *confined,* you are kept within limits. *Firm* means "supported," so *confirm* means "to give support to," or " to verify."

Finally, before some words or roots the *con-* and *com-* prefix is spelled *col-*. The word *collaborate,* for example, means "to work together," and *collate* means "to gather together in a proper order."

Word Part	Meaning	English Word
com-, con-, col-	together; with	combine, confined, collaborate,
fort	strong	comfort
plere	to fill	complete

Finding Meanings

Write each word or word part below beside its meaning.

confirm **col-** **forte** **compose** **complete**

1. with; together ______________________
2. in a loud or forceful manner ______________________
3. verify ______________________
4. finished; whole; full ______________________
5. to put together ______________________

True or False

Write T if a statement is true or F if it is false.

__________ 1. If you have a collection of seashells, you have a group of one thing.

__________ 2. To complete a race is to begin at the starting line.

__________ 3. When you compose your written assignments, you put together your ideas, and then write them down.

__________ 4. Since *con-* means "together," and *vent* comes from a root that means "to come," a convention is a coming together of a group of people.

__________ 5. The notation *forte* on a piece of sheet music tells the pianist to play fast.

Answering Questions

1. If you work together on a project with a large group, you have to ____________________

____

2 When you are upset and someone tells you to "pull yourself together," or to "get yourself together," they are telling you to ____________________ yourself.

3. To make the color orange, what two colors need to be combined?____________________

____

4. In order for this sentence to be finished, you have to ____________________ it by filling in the blank.

5. If you know *con-* means "together" and *greg* means "to collect into a crowd," what do you think *congregate* means? ____

____

1-4 Review and Extension

Multiple Meanings

Some of the vocabulary words you studied in lessons 1 and 3 have more than one meaning. Read each word listed below and its definitions. Next to each sentence that follows, write the letter of the definition that matches the meaning of the word as it is used in that sentence.

graduate

a. (v.) to finish a course of study at school
b. (v.) to pass from one stage or level to a higher one
c. (v.) to mark out in equal spaces for measuring

seasoned

a. (v.) improved the flavor of
b. (adj.) grown experienced over a period of time
c. (v.) made fit or became fit by treatment or aging

fold

a. (v.) to bend or double over on itself
b. (v.) to bring to an end; go out of business

_________ 1. The soup was delicious, **seasoned** with just the right combination of fresh herbs from the garden.

_________ 2. The track is **graduated** in 10-yard sections, so runners can easily calculate their speed and distance.

_________ 3. After three summers as a stock boy at the supermarket, Lloyd finally **graduated** to the position of clerk.

_________ 4. The roller-skating rink **folded** without warning; one day it was filled with skaters, and the next a For Sale sign was posted.

_________ 5. A cast-iron skillet should be **seasoned** with oil every few months to ensure a smooth, slippery surface for cooking.

_________ 6. Before he raced off to soccer practice, William **folded** his shirts and put them into the drawer.

_________ 7. Irene was genuinely surprised to find out that she would **graduate** from college with the highest honors.

Word Parts Review

Complete each sentence so that it makes sense and shows the meaning of the boldfaced vocabulary word.

1. The blue paint was **combined** ______________________________

   ____

2. In an attempt to offer **comfort,** Frank ______________________________

   ____

3. The teacher **postponed** the test, so that she ______________________________

   ____

4. After Anna **completed** the test, she felt ______________________________

   ____

5. Since the woman **preceded** him in the ticket line, she would ______________________________

   ____

6. In preparing for the **convention,** the hotel management ______________________________

   ____

7. "If this meat has been **precooked,**" Elmer began, "then ______________________________

   ____

8. The **postscript** described how the author ______________________________

   ____

9. Since he was **confined** to his room all weekend, Luis ______________________________

   ____

10. From the way he spoke, it was clear that John was **prejudiced** ______________________________

    ____

Synonym Study

Following are synonym studies for two vocabulary words you studied in lessons 1 and 3. Use either the vocabulary words or their synonyms to complete the sentences in this exercise. Refer to the synonym studies as you decide which choice best fits the context of each sentence.

attain **acquire**

The words *attain* and *acquire* both mean "to gain or reach." Attain is used when speaking of accomplishment or of reaching a particular state of being. *She attained her goal. The man had attained the ripe old age of 90.* Acquire means to come into possession of a material object or a personality trait or characteristic by one of any number of different means. *Morgan acquired a limp in his youth. Upon the death of her grandfather, Kate acquired his estate.*

1. Penelope could not remember how she had ________________________ the antique Oriental vase on the table in her parlor.

2. Maureen worked hard to ________________________ the balance she wanted between her social life and her studies.

3. Over the years, Hernandez ________________________ an annoying habit of clicking his teeth after every few words of conversation.

4. The leaders of the two nations were responsible to their people for finding a way to ________________________ peace.

distinctive **peculiar**

Distinctive and *peculiar* both indicate a special quality. A distinctive quality is one that is noticeably different and uncommon. It is often special in the sense of being superior or worthy of notice. *Her paintings had a distinctive brightness.* Peculiar applies to qualities belonging only to an individual, a group, or a certain kind of thing. It stresses an unusual quality and sometimes implies strangeness or oddness as well. *He spoke in an accent peculiar to the eastern hills of Tennessee.*

5. The house was painted a ________________________ shade of blue, which gave it a stately, handsome look.

6. Roy's dog had a ________________________ odor that made him unpopular among the neighborhood's pets.

7. In Tibet, archaeologists found remnants of cave paintings ________________ to an ancient tribe of nomads.

8. The actor was known for his romantic good looks and ________________ walk.

Word Forms

The words listed below are other forms of the vocabulary words you worked with in lessons 1 and 3. Fill in the blank in each sentence with the appropriate word. If you are unsure of the meaning of a word, look it up in the glossary.

attainment **graduation** **folding** **distinction** **confine** **attainable**

1. The naked eye is not capable of seeing the ________________ between minute differences in size.
2. Paul's main goal was the ________________ of a degree in architecture.
3. For the first time in her 10 long years of training, Michelle believed that her dream of becoming a distinguished opera singer was ________________
4. The discouraged partners racked their brains trying to think of something that might keep their catering business from ________________
5. Greg intended to take a vacation after ________________ and then start searching for a job.
6. The speaker asked that we ________________ our questions to the subject of the school budget.
7. Lida's uncle received a medal for serving his country with ________________ in Vietnam.
8. Arnetta tried ________________ the poster in half, but the paper was too stiff.
9. My mom threatened to ________________ me to my room if I didn't finish my homework before I started watching TV.
10. Many of the spectators at the parade brought their own ________________ chairs.

Using Your Vocabulary

The scrambled words below are vocabulary words from lessons 1–4. Use the definition or synonym next to each scramble to help you figure out what the word is. Then write the word on the lines provided. The circled letters will form a phrase related to golf. Write that phrase on the line at the bottom of the puzzle.

1. OMEPSCO	formulate	_ _ _ _ _ ◯ _
2. NIBORUTILAT	distress	_ _ _ _ _ ◯ _ _ _ _ _
3. CADEED	ten years	_ _ _ ◯ _ _
4. CREPDEE	go ahead of	◯ _ _ _ _ _ _
5. DTUENDRYSU	substitute	_ _ _ _ _ ◯ _ _ _ _
6. TODIICN	pronunciation	_ _ _ ◯ _ _ _
7. BNOCMEI	blend	_ _ _ _ ◯ _ _
8. RAQECUI	get	_ ◯ _ _ _ _ _
9. OPERKCO	cook ahead	_ _ _ _ _ _ ◯
10. RTPIHEOSRCI	before written history	_ _ _ ◯ _ _ _ _ _ _ _
11. POTERU	acting company	_ _ _ ◯ _ _
12. OLTECMPE	finish	_ _ ◯ _ _ _ _ _
13. NEDSSAOE	experienced	_ _ _ _ ◯ _ _ _
14. ERALIPUC	odd	_ _ _ _ _ _ _ ◯

Phrase: ______________________________

Word Play

Palindromes

Backward and forward they read the same. They get their name from the Greek word *palindromos,* meaning "running back again." A palindrome may consist of a single word, such as *madam,* or a phrase or sentence—Madam, I'm Adam.

People who enjoy playing with words have been making up palindromes for thousands of years. A famous Greek palindrome that appears around many water fountains reads

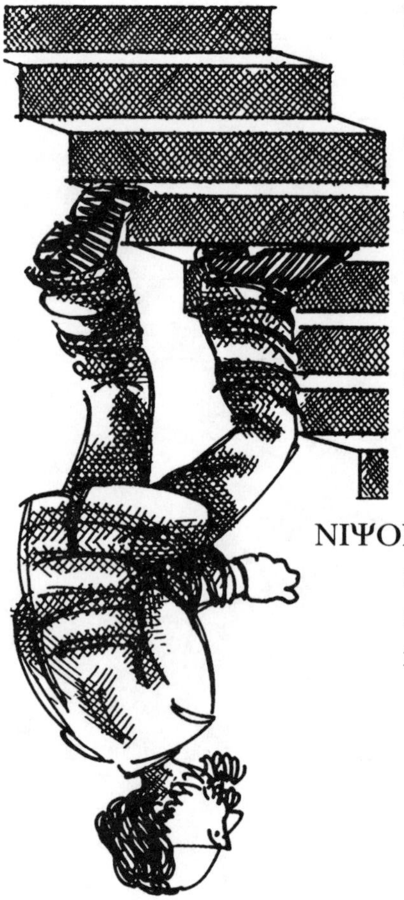

NIΨONANOMHMATAMHMONANOΨIN

meaning "Wash my transgressions, not only my face."

Below are a few well-known palindromes. In the last one, each word is a palindrome as well. Can you compose a palindrome of your own?

Step on no pets.
A man, a plan, a canal—Panama.
Never odd or even.
Anna: "Did Otto peep?" Otto: "Did Anna?"

5 Cat Communication

Cats communicate with one another, with other animals, and with human beings in a variety of ways. Cats use sounds, body signals, and scents as means of communication.

Some experts estimate that a cat can make more than 60 different sounds, ranging from a soft purr to a loud wail, or *caterwaul.* These sounds **originate** in the *larynx* (voice box) in the throat. Cats can purr on both *inspiration* (breathing in) and *expiration* (breathing out). The sound is produced by air as it vibrates through the space in the larynx called the *glottis.*

The sounds a cat makes may have various meanings. For example, depending on the situation, a meow can be a friendly greeting, or it may express curiosity, hunger, or loneliness. Purring usually means contentment, but some cats also purr when they are sick. Hisses, growls, and screams **indicate** anger and fear.

Cats also communicate through various body and tail positions and facial expressions. A contented cat often lies on its chest with its eyes half closed. To invite play or petting, some cats roll over on one side and wave a paw in the air. However, a similar **posture** accompanied by extended claws, a **direct** stare, and ears folded back indicates a fearful cat ready to defend itself. A friendly cat may greet someone with its tail raised vertically. It may also bump its head against the person and lick an extended hand. An angry or frightened cat flicks its tail from side to side, arches its back, and puffs up its fur. A **submissive** cat crouches down, flattens its ears, and avoids direct eye contact.

Personal Words

Choose two words from the selection that are unfamiliar to you or whose meanings you are not completely sure of. (Do not choose words that appear in boldfaced type.) Write the words on the lines provided. Beside each word write what you think it means, based on how it was used in the selection.

1. ____________________ : ____

____

2. ____________________ : ____

____

Using Context

Put an **X** in the box beside the best definition for each boldfaced word. For clues to the meanings of words, reread the parts of the passage in which they appear.

1. These sounds **originate** in the larynx (voice box) in the throat.
   - ☐ a. grow
   - ☐ b. begin
   - ☐ c. continue
   - ☐ d. stay
2. However, a similar posture accompanied by extended claws, a **direct** stare, and ears folded back indicates a fearful cat ready to defend itself.
   - ☐ a. straightforward
   - ☐ b. timid
   - ☐ c. brief
   - ☐ d. unsteady
3. Hisses, growls, and screams **indicate** anger and fear.
   - ☐ a. eliminate
   - ☐ b. take the place of
   - ☐ c. cause
   - ☐ d. are a sign of
4. However, a similar **posture** accompanied by extended claws, a direct stare, and ears folded back indicates a fearful cat ready to defend itself.
   - ☐ a. game
   - ☐ b. greeting
   - ☐ c. body position
   - ☐ d. walk
5. A **submissive** cat crouches down, flattens its ears, and avoids direct eye contact.
   - ☐ a. yielding to authority
   - ☐ b. poorly trained
   - ☐ c. excited and playful
   - ☐ d. sick

Making Connections

A On the line next to each word or phrase, write the vocabulary word that is related to it. The related word may be a synonym, an antonym, or a definition for the vocabulary word.

originate **direct** **indicate** **posture** **submissive**

1. signify ______________________
2. rebellious ______________________
3. bold ______________________
4. stance ______________________
5. gives in easily ______________________
6. start out ______________________
7. point out ______________________
8. end up ______________________
9. obedient ______________________
10. position ______________________

B Complete the following analogies by inserting one of the five vocabulary words in the blank at the end of each one. In an analogy, the last two words or phrases must be related to each other in the same way that the first two are related. The colon in an analogy is read "is to," and the symbol :: is read "as."

originate **direct** **indicate** **posture** **submissive**

1. wave : greet : : point : ________________
2. see: observe : :obedient : ________________
3. happy : sad : : roundabout : ________________
4. curved : straight : : end : ________________
5. face : expression : : body : ________________

C Complete each sentence with the correct vocabulary word.

originate **direct** **indicate** **posture** **submissive**

1. Gloria's erect ________________ makes her appear taller than she actually is.
2. Manny asked a ________________ question and was rewarded with an equally straightforward answer.
3. Randy, a ________________ child, climbed the fence when his brother told him to, even though he was scared.
4. The signal beside the tracks turned yellow to ________________ that a train was approaching.
5. The cacao tree, from whose seeds chocolate and cocoa are made,

   ________________ in the West Indies.

Personal Words Follow-up

Use a dictionary to find the definitions for the personal words you chose at the beginning of this lesson. If a word has more than one meaning, look for the meaning that defines the word as it is used in the selection. Then write the words and their dictionary definitions in the Personal Words pages at the back of the book. How close did you come to figuring out their meanings for yourself?

6 Word Study

The Latin word part *ad-* means "to" or "toward." The word *adhere* means "to stick fast" or "to cling." The root *here* comes from a Latin word meaning "to stick." *Adhesive* tape adheres to almost any surface. *Adhere* also means "to support a person or an idea"—to be loyal. Someone who adheres to certain ideas or beliefs sticks by them. The root *apt* means "to fit," so to adapt something is to make it fit, often by modifying it to some extent. The root *jac* or *jec* means "lie." The word *adjacent* means "to lie next to or close by." So buildings that are adjacent are, literally, lying next to each other.

When *ad-* appears before a word or root beginning with *c,* its spelling changes to *ac-*. For example, the word *accent* means "a greater stress given to a particular syllable or word in speech." *Accentuate* also means "to emphasize or stress something."

When *ad-* is used with a word beginning with *f,* its spelling changes to *af-,* as in *affirm.* To affirm means to approve or state firmly. Someone who is an *affiliate* is connected closely to an association.

Word Part	Meaning	English Word
ad-, ac-, af-	to; toward	adapt, accent, affirm
apt	to fit	adapt
here	to stick	adherent
jac, jec	to lie	adjacent

Finding Meanings

Write each word or word part beside its meaning.

adhere **affirm** **adjacent** **accent** **adherent**

1. to stress; emphasize ____________________
2. to stick fast; to cling ____________________
3. to approve; to declare ____________________
4. next to; close by ____________________
5. a firm supporter who sticks by an idea or cause ____________________

True or False

Write T if a statement is true or F if it is false.

__________ 1. If your house and your best friend's house are adjacent, you are next-door neighbors.

__________ 2. To affirm means to give approval or agree to do something.

__________ 3. If you accent part of a word, you are not emphasizing it strongly.

__________ 4. Glue can be used to adhere the parts of a model airplane to one another.

__________ 5. Adherents of an idea are those people who oppose the idea.

Choose an Answer

Put an **X** in front of the answer choice you think is correct.

1. If someone moves to a new country and feels comfortable, it could be said that she has
   - ☐ a. affirmed new things.
   - ☐ b. adhered to her ways.
   - ☐ c. adapted to a new life.

2. When the workers went on strike, they hoped their problems would be
   - ☐ a. accentuated.
   - ☐ b. accessed.
   - ☐ c. adherent.

3. A group that is connected to a larger organization would be called an
   - ☐ a. adhesion.
   - ☐ b. affiliate.
   - ☐ c. accent.

4. Flies stick to flypaper because the paper is coated with a substance that makes them
   - ☐ a. sick.
   - ☐ b. fit.
   - ☐ c. adhere.

5. Two countries located on either side of the same border are
   - ☐ a. adherents.
   - ☐ b. adjacent.
   - ☐ c. parallel.

7 Caring for a Cat

Cats are clean animals and easy to housebreak. To train a cat to use a litter box, one must watch the animal carefully. When it begins to wander searchingly from one place to another, it must be put into the litter box. The litter must be changed often, and the pan should be washed with soap and water every few days.

A cat likes to exercise its claws by digging them into or scratching furniture. A scratching post helps to **reduce** damage to furniture. A piece of wood covered with carpeting makes a good scratching post. Every time the cat claws at the furniture, it should be taken to the post, until it learns to use it on its own.

Most cats refuse to be **disciplined,** although they may understand "no." They learn their names quickly, however, and many will come when called. If a cat is shown a trick that it likes, it will learn to do it.

Cats should be **confined** to the house, especially at night. Cats that are allowed to roam disturb the neighbors with their crying and fighting. A female cat should never be allowed to roam during her mating season.

Proper care usually will **eliminate** the threat of disease. Unusual symptoms or behavior should be watched for, and the animal should be taken to the veterinarian on a regular basis. A cat should be vaccinated early against rabies and other serious diseases.

A cat will clean itself by licking its fur. As it licks itself, it will swallow hairs that eventually form feltlike balls in its stomach and intestines. Although daily brushing cuts down on hair balls, some will form anyway. A veterinarian can prescribe a **remedy** to help a cat eliminate the hair.

Lastly, a cat should never be dropped or thrown, as it can be seriously injured. Contrary to popular belief, cats do not always land on their feet.

Personal Words

Choose two words from the selection that are unfamiliar to you or whose meanings you are not completely sure of. (Do not choose words that appear in boldfaced type.) Write the words on the lines provided. Beside each word write what you think it means, based on how it was used in the selection.

1. ________________ : ____________________________________

____

2. ________________ : ____________________________________

____

Using Context

Put an **X** in the box beside each correct answer. For clues to the meanings of the boldfaced words, reread the parts of the passage in which they appear.

1. From the sentence in which *remedy* appears, you can tell that a **remedy** prescribed by a veterinarian is a
   - ☐ a. friend.
   - ☐ b. medication.
   - ☐ c. hairbrush.
   - ☐ d. special exercise.

2. To "**eliminate** the threat" of disease or injury means to
   - ☐ a. get rid of the possibility.
   - ☐ b. lessen the seriousness.
   - ☐ c. change the course.
   - ☐ d. increase the chances.

3. A cat who is "**confined** to the house" is one that
   - ☐ a. doesn't have a home.
   - ☐ b. doesn't like to go outside.
   - ☐ c. is sick.
   - ☐ d. is not allowed to go outside.

4. The sentence in which **disciplined** appears helps you to understand that in this context the word means
   - ☐ a. trained to obey.
   - ☐ b. put out of the house.
   - ☐ c. punished.
   - ☐ d. yelled at.

5. The sentence in which the word **reduce** appears tells you that if you provide a scratching post for your cat, damage to your furniture will be
   - ☐ a. repaired.
   - ☐ b. lessened.
   - ☐ c. increased.
   - ☐ d. delayed.

Making Connections

A Complete the following analogies by inserting one of the five vocabulary words in the blank at the end of each one. Remember that in an analogy, the last two words or phrases must be related in the same way that the first two are related.

remedy **eliminate** **confine** **discipline** **reduce**

1. make worse : improve : : create : ____________________
2. bath soap : cleanser : : aspirin : ____________________
3. eat : appetite : : behave : ____________________
4. collide : crash : : diminish : ____________________
5. caretaker : tend : : jailer : ____________________

B On the line beside each sentence, write the vocabulary word that has the same meaning as the underlined word or words.

remedy **eliminate** **confined** **disciplined** **reduce**

1. ______________________ Mary Ellen's cat had been trained to behave properly from the time it was a kitten.
2. ______________________ When baking brownies, Gale decided to leave out the walnuts because her friend Liz was allergic to them.
3. ______________________ The school yearbook was printed in black and white instead of color, in order to lower the printing costs.
4. ______________________ Pamela was unable to leave the house for two weeks when she had pneumonia.
5. ______________________ Native Americans gave the colonists a simple medicine that they used to fight the fevers that were common.

C Complete each sentence with the correct vocabulary word.

remedy **eliminate** **confined** **disciplined** **reduce**

1. Reggie was ______________________ to his bedroom all evening as punishment for the fight he started with his brother.
2. A well-known ______________________ for hiccups is to breathe into a paper bag.
3. Mrs. Grossman ______________________ her students effectively without any yelling or threats.
4. A proposal to ______________________ the official number of school days from 180 to 165 was brought before the committee.
5. Carol decided to ______________________ ice cream, candy, and baked goods from her diet in order to try to lose 10 pounds.

Personal Words Follow-up

Use a dictionary to find the definitions for the personal words you chose at the beginning of this lesson. If a word has more than one meaning, look for the meaning that defines the word as it is used in the selection. Then write the words and their dictionary definitions in the Personal Words pages at the back of the book. How close did you come to figuring out their meanings for yourself?

8 Word Study

The prefix *dis-*, meaning "not" or "the opposite of" is attached to the beginning of many English words to form new words. *Disagree,* for example, means "not to agree" and *discontinue,* means "to stop doing something."

The root word *orient* may mean either "to arrange something in the proper way" or "to get one's bearings." To be disoriented means to have lost your sense of direction or your sense of time or place. *Lodge* means "to get caught" or "to stay in place." *Dislodge,* therefore, means "to force out of place," or "to get something unstuck."

The prefix *de-* has a number of meanings, all having to do with undoing. To *decode* means to take out of code. *Decompose* means the opposite of *compose.* So something that has decomposed has rotted, or has been separated into its basic elements. *Deduct* means "to lead away or take away." The *duc* part of deduct comes from the Latin *ducere,* meaning "to lead." When *de-* is added to another root, *tract,* we have *detract,* which means "to draw away or take away a part of something."

Word Part	Meaning	English Word
dis-	not; the opposite of; from	disagree, discontinue
orient	to arrange; to get one's bearings	disorient
lodge	to get caught; to stay in place	dislodge
de-	remove; reduce; get off; do the opposite of	decode, decompose
duc	to lead	deduct
tract	to draw	detract

Finding Meanings

Write each word or word part beside its meaning.

dis- **de-** **duc** **orient** **lodge**

1. not; the opposite of ____________________
2. to stay in place ____________________
3. to arrange in the proper way ____________________
4. to lead ____________________
5. remove from; reduce; do the opposite of ____________________

True or False

Write T if a statement is true or F if it is false.

_________ 1. A television series that has been discontinued will be back on the air the next season.

_________ 2. When matter separates into its basic elements, it decomposes.

_________ 3. A badminton birdie that is stuck in the net is lodged there.

_________ 4. Many deductions make a paycheck larger.

_________ 5. When two people feel, think, and talk about something in exactly the same way, they are having a disagreement.

Answering Questions

1. If someone dislodges a bird's nest, what has that person done? _______________________

____

2. If you were to deduct $50 from $100, how much money would you have? _______________

____

3. *Dis-* means "not" and *aster* means "star." What word from the 16th century described what was believed could happen if the stars and planets were arranged in an unlucky way?

____

4. If *ease* means "freedom from pain or discomfort," what does it mean to have a disease?

____

5. What does it mean to say that a train has been derailed? _______________________

____

5-8 Review and Extension

Multiple Meanings

Some of the vocabulary words you studied in lessons 5 and 7 have more than one meaning. Complete each sentence in this exercise with a vocabulary word from the list below. In these sentences, the words have different meanings than they had in the selection you read. If you are unsure of the various meanings of a word, look it up in the glossary.

disciplined **posture** **reduced** **originated**

1. The snow was ________________________ to a slushy mess after a few hours of warm sunshine.
2. The ancient Romans, who ran hot-water pipes beneath their stone floors, ________________________ the idea of central heating.
3. In current events class, Mr. Valentino asked for opinions on the present ________________________ of the country in terms of foreign policy.
4. Leonard laughed so hard at the Marx Brothers movie that he was ________________________ to tears.
5. Marie was severely ________________________ for getting home two hours past her curfew.
6. The plan to collect money for the homeless shelter ________________________ with the high school's student council.

Word Parts Review

Complete each sentence so that it makes sense and shows the meaning of the boldfaced vocabulary word.

1. When Tom **discontinued** his trumpet lessons ____

____

2. To **decode** the message, which was written in numbers, Lou had to ____________________

____

3. The boys **adapted** the rules of the game so that ______________________________

____

4. Charlie wanted to sit **adjacent** to Ted, so he ______________________________

____

5. Jack became **disoriented** when ______________________________

____

6. To **orient** herself in the woods, Gretchen ______________________________

____

7. To make the fruits and vegetables **decompose** faster, Adam______________________

____

8. Because the stamp wouldn't **adhere,** ______________________________

____

9. Though Micky tried and tried to **dislodge** the stone, ______________________

____

10. When Stephanie read her pay stub, she was amazed that the **deductions** __________

____

Synonym Study

Following are synonym studies for three vocabulary words you studied in lessons 5 and 7. Use either the vocabulary words or their synonyms to complete the sentences in this exercise. Refer to the synonym studies as you decide which choice best fits the context of each sentence.

confine **limit**

Confine and *limit* both mean "to set bounds for." Confine suggests severe limitations—being kept or held in. *Marjorie was confined to her room for the evening because she had not done her chores. Jack is confined to a low-level job because of lack of education.* Limit implies setting a point or line beyond which something cannot or is not allowed to go. A limit may be set in time, space, speed, or degree. *The airplane's speed is limited by the power of its engines. The time limit on the test is 20 minutes.*

1. When Jeanne dances, she ________________________ her movements to the upper part of her body.

2. Mrs. Gantry asked Matthew to ________________________ his thoughts to issues of grammar while in English class, instead of daydreaming about other things.

3. While working on an assembly line in a candy factory, Ellen was

   ________________________ to a space about four feet square.

submissive **obedient**

Submissive and *obedient* describe people who are doing what they've been told to do. A submissive person continually gives in to what other people want, while an obedient person simply follows rules set by an authority.

4. In his large family, Benjamin found it easier to be ________________________ than to stand up for his own rights.

5. Most drivers are ________________________ and stop for red lights.

originate **begin**

Originate and *begin* both have to do with a starting point. To begin means to start or to do the first part of something. To originate means to come into existence or to be born. *The idea originated in a small laboratory in France.*

6. The play *Charles DeGaulle in France* ________________________ with a scene on a battlefield in Normandy.

7. The paper company ________________________ in San Francisco over 40 years ago.

8. Marc wondered where the folktale about the boy and the elephant

   ________________________.

Word Forms

The words listed below are other forms of the vocabulary words you worked with in lessons 5 and 7. Fill in the blank in each sentence with the appropriate word. If you are unsure of the meaning of a word, look it up in the glossary.

origin	**indication**	**submit**	**reduction**
discipline	**confines**	**remedied**	

1. The strict ________________________ within the Robinson household left little room for fun and games.
2. Tracy learned that she had to ________________________ to the coach's rules in order to remain on the track team.
3. Seeing Helen's fear of the dog, Jim ________________________ the situation by putting the animal in the house.
4. When Tracy heard of the tradition of buttering people's noses on their birthdays, she wondered what the ________________________ of the strange practice could have been.
5. In the ________________________ of his room, Marco could relax and forget about what other people expected of him.
6. The shoes were expensive, so Beverly waited two weeks for a further ________________________ in the price before buying them.
7. The sharp, cold air provided a clear ________________________ that winter was just around the corner.

Using Your Vocabulary

Use vocabulary words from lessons 1–8 to complete the crossword puzzle.

ACROSS

3. obediently passive
5. uneasiness
6. get rid of
8. change to fit or to make work
10. confused about which direction to go in
12. group of fans
13. begin
15. consequence
16. custom

DOWN

1. does as told
2. double over on itself
3. give in
4. sign
7. sticky substance
9. great misfortune
11. crack a code
14. reach

Word Play

Pleasure or Punishment?

It is sometimes said that puns are the lowest form of humor, but that is only true of bad puns. A good pun is clever and holds the delightful element of surprise that is the foundation of all good jokes.

A pun is usually defined as a play on words, but that definition isn't very satisfactory. Just what is a play on words? Well, of course puns are word jokes —the key words themselves are humorous in some way. But what makes them so? The basis of every pun is a word or a phrase that has a double meaning. In a truly good pun, both meanings make sense, and the mind goes back and forth between the two meanings.

William Shakespeare, a great wordsmith if ever there was one, could manufacture an admirable pun. In *Julius Caesar,* he presented a cobbler who says that he is "a mender of bad soles." The homonym of *soles—souls* creates the pun. The same cobbler says that he meddles "with no tradesman's matters, nor women's matters, but with awl." Here the pun is on the word *awl.* An awl is a pointed tool used by a cobbler to make holes in leather, and its name is a homonym of *all,* meaning "everything."

Some less-literary puns appear below. You can judge for yourself whether they are good or bad. If your reaction is a groan rather than a grin, you can be pretty sure that the pun is approaching the lower end of the humor scale.

Two ghosts drifted into a tavern and asked the bartender, "Do you serve spirits here?"

When a group of miniature cattle were put in *Sputnik,* it became the herd shot round the world.

Once a hunter in the woods lost his dog, so he put an ear to a tree and listened to the bark.

The big firecracker said to the little firecracker, "My pop's bigger than your pop!"

"Don't tell me. You guys want to report another beating, right?"

9 The Birth of Aviation

Kitty Hawk and Kill Devil Hill are American place names that will live in history. There Wilbur and Orville Wright made the world's first successful flight of a heavier-than-air, manned, power-driven machine.

On December 17, 1903, the machine was flown with a person on board for the first time. It was a cold and windy morning when Orville Wright climbed aboard the plane. His first power-driven flight, a distance of 120 feet, lasted just 12 seconds. From that achievement of the Wrights, the science of aeronautics developed.

Wilbur and Orville started out selling bicycles. They formed the Wright Cycle Company in 1892. Business was good, and they soon added a repair shop. The brothers twice moved their growing business to larger quarters. As a next step, they began to manufacture bicycles. Eventually they came up with a low-priced model known as the Wright Special. They manufactured several hundred Wright Specials before **discontinuing** the business in order to **devote** full time to aviation.

Repairing and manufacturing bicycles sharpened the brothers' mechanical skills. In their construction of flying machines, Wilbur and Orville often used the same equipment and tools they used to repair bicycles. They **conducted** many experiments in the back room of their shop, and most of the parts used in the first successful airplane were built there.

Despite their devotion to hard work, Wilbur and Orville found time for the lighter side of life. They were not long-faced and **stern** but **sprightly** and good-humored. They loved small children and dogs, music, and practical jokes. Close companions in their personal lives as well as in business, the brothers shared everything.

Personal Words

Choose two words from the selection that are unfamiliar to you or whose meanings you are not completely sure of. (Do not choose words that appear in boldfaced type.) Write the words on the lines provided. Beside each word write what you think it means, based on how it was used in the selection.

1. ____________________ : ____

____

2. ____________________ : ____

____

Using Context

Go back and read the paragraph in which each word appears, paying special attention to the sentence in which it is used. Then circle the word that has the same or almost the same meaning. Be prepared to support your choices.

1. **discontinuing**	waiting	running	stopping	starting
2. **devote**	elect	give	sell	divide
3. **conducted**	guided	proved	played	mixed
4. **stern**	happy	serious	kind	healthy
5. **sprightly**	slow	old	energetic	beautiful

Making Connections

A Write each word from the list below beside its definition. To figure out what each word means, go back to the passage and read the sentence that contains the word. If you can't discover the meaning from the way the word is used in the sentence, read the sentences that come before and after it for clues.

discontinue **devote** **conducted** **stern** **sprightly**

1. ____________________ performed; carried on
2. ____________________ put an end to
3. ____________________ severe; harsh
4. ____________________ lively; spirited
5. ____________________ give full attention to

B Complete the following analogies by inserting one of the five vocabulary words in the blank at the end of each one. Remember that in an analogy the last two words or phrases must be related to each other in the same way that the first two are related. The colon in an analogy is read "is to," and the symbol :: is read "as." So high : low : : wide : narrow is read "high is to low as wide is to narrow."

discontinue **devote** **conducted** **stern** **sprightly**

1. write : print : : stop : ____________________
2. happy : funny : : serious : ____________________
3. runner : fast : : elf : ____________________
4. cake : bake : : experiment : ____________________
5. detest : adore : : neglect : ____________________

C Complete each sentence with the correct vocabulary word.

discontinue **devote** **conducted** **stern** **sprightly**

1. To help visitors learn about the wonders of the pine forest, the park offers nature walks ____________________ by trained guides.
2. Though he just celebrated his 90th birthday, Mr. Borden remains unusually alert and ____________________
3. After failing math, John promised his parents he would ____________________ more time and energy to his studies.
4. Mrs. Joel's ____________________ face, with her tight lips and disapproving eyes, told Henry that she was not pleased to find him digging for worms in her front yard.
5. The bookstore's policy is to ____________________ any book that sells fewer than two copies a year.

Personal Words Follow-up

Use a dictionary to find the definitions for the personal words you chose at the beginning of this lesson. If a word has more than one meaning, look for the meaning that defines the word as it is used in the story. Then write the words and their dictionary definitions in the Personal Words pages at the back of the book. How close did you come to figuring out their meanings for yourself?

10 Word Study

You already use many words that contain the prefix *un-*, which means "not" or "the opposite of." If you are no longer happy, you are unhappy. Someone who is uncivilized is not civilized or not polite.

There are many other prefixes that mean "not." The prefix *in-* is another way of expressing the opposite of a base word. *Incorrect,* for example, means "not correct." If you are not capable of doing something, you are incapable. The prefixes *im-* and *il-* are variations of *in-*. *Im-* is used before words starting with the letter *m* or *p*. *Im-* means "not" in such words as *impossible* (not possible), *improper* (not proper), or *immobile* (not moving). *Il-* is used with roots beginning with the letter *l*. To be unable to read or write is to be illiterate. Something that is not legal is illegal. The prefixes *in-* and *im-* can also mean "inside." *Inhabit* means "to live in." Someone who is put in prison is imprisoned.

Another negative prefix is *non-*. It can mean "not," "the opposite of," or "the lack of." *Nonsense* means "not making sense." A nonprofit organization does not make a profit beyond what it needs to run the organization.

Word Part	Meaning	English Word
un-	not; the opposite of	unhappy, uncivilized
in-, im-	not; the opposite of;	incorrect, impossible
	inside	inhabited, imprisoned
il-	not	illiterate, illegal
non-	not; the opposite of	nonsense, nonprofit

Finding Meanings

Write each word or word part beside its meaning.

un- **impossible** **nonsense** **incapable** **illiterate**

1. not possible ____________________
2. not able ____________________
3. not able to read or write ____________________
4. opposite of ____________________
5. talk or action that makes no sense ____________________

True or False

Write T if a statement is true or F if it is false.

__________ 1. An illegible contract is one that can be read easily.

__________ 2. An inhabited building has people living in it.

__________ 3. Someone with a broken leg is incapable of dancing.

__________ 4. Many nonprofit groups do work that helps poor people.

__________ 5. The best readers are illiterate.

Choose an Answer

Put an **X** in front of the answer choice you think is correct.

1. An answer that lacks good sense is
   - ☐ a. illiterate.
   - ☐ b. illegal.
   - ☐ c. illogical.
2. Someone who is angry is
   - ☐ a. humorous.
   - ☐ b. ill-humored.
   - ☐ c. inhuman.
3. Driving faster than the speed limit is
   - ☐ a. illegal.
   - ☐ b. illegible.
   - ☐ c. illogical.
4. Someone who wears jeans to a formal party is dressed
   - ☐ a. importantly.
   - ☐ b. impossibly.
   - ☐ c. improperly.
5. The convicted criminal was immediately
   - ☐ a. imposed.
   - ☐ b. improved.
   - ☐ c. imprisoned.

11 With the Greatest of Ease

Orville Wright made his first public flight on September 3, 1908, at Fort Myer, Virginia. He was testing an airplane for possible use by the U.S. government. He circled the field one and one-half times on the first test. Theodore Roosevelt Jr. is reported to have said, "When the plane first rose, the crowd's gasp of surprise was not alone at the wonder of it, but because it was so unexpected." Orville's last flight at Fort Myer in 1908 ended in tragedy. The airplane crashed, killing Lt. Thomas Selfridge, a passenger. Orville himself **sustained** broken ribs, a fractured leg, and hip injuries.

In 1909, Orville completed the government test flights by flying just under 43 miles an hour. The United States Army **formally** accepted its first airplane from the Wrights on August 2, 1909. During the same year, the brothers enjoyed further flying triumphs both in Europe and at home. While Orville was making great flights in Germany, Wilbur was doing the same in New York.

The brothers established their first airplane manufacturing companies in France and Germany. Later the Wright Company was organized in the United States as well, with Wilbur as president and Orville as vice president. In financial affairs the Wrights were surprisingly **shrewd.** But though they became wealthy and famous, they did not feel **fulfilled** as businessmen. They looked forward to the time when they could retire and spend their days doing scientific research.

Orville returned to Kill Devil Hill in October 1911 to experiment with an automatic control device and to make soaring flights with a glider. On October 24 he set a new world record for soaring, which was not **exceeded** until ten years later. On May 30, 1912, Wilbur Wright died of typhoid fever at the age of 45. Orville outlived him by 36 years.

Personal Words

Choose two words from the selection that are unfamiliar to you or whose meanings you are not completely sure of. (Do not choose words that appear in boldfaced type.) Write the words on the lines provided. Beside each word write what you think it means, based on how it was used in the selection.

1. ______________________ : ____

____

2. ______________________ : ____

____

Using Context

Put an **X** in the box beside the best definition for each boldfaced word. For clues to the meanings of words, reread the parts of the passage in which they appear.

1. Orville himself **sustained** broken ribs, a fractured leg, and hip injuries.
   - ☐ a. got away with
   - ☐ b. experienced
   - ☐ c. hated
   - ☐ d. caused

2. The United States Army **formally** accepted its first airplane from the Wrights on August 2, 1909.
   - ☐ a. later
   - ☐ b. happily
   - ☐ c. officially
   - ☐ d. finally

3. In financial affairs the Wrights were surprisingly **shrewd.**
   - ☐ a. sharp minded
   - ☐ b. lazy
   - ☐ c. stupid
   - ☐ d. innocent

4. But though they became wealthy and famous, they did not feel **fulfilled** as businessmen.
   - ☐ a. excited
   - ☐ b. capable
   - ☐ c. satisfied
   - ☐ d. respected

5. On October 24 he set a new world record for soaring, which was not **exceeded** until ten years later.
   - ☐ a. topped
   - ☐ b. recorded
   - ☐ c. noticed
   - ☐ d. lowered

Making Connections

A On the line next to each word or phrase, write the vocabulary word that is related to it. The related word may be a synonym, an antonym, or a definition for the vocabulary word.

sustained **formally** **shrewd** **fulfilled** **exceeded**

1. intelligent ______________________
2. dissatisfied ______________________
3. surpassed ______________________
4. underwent ______________________
5. with ceremony______________________
6. outdid ______________________
7. dull ______________________
8. casually ______________________
9. went beyond ______________________
10. complete ______________________

B On the line in front of each sentence, write the vocabulary word that has the same meaning as the underlined word or words.

sustained **formally** **shrewd** **fulfilled** **exceeded**

1. ______________________ The keenly perceptive observations that Nina expressed in her essay greatly impressed her teacher.
2. ______________________ In the track meet, Donald surpassed the previous high school record for the forty-yard dash.
3. ______________________ The car was totaled in the crash, and Janet suffered a bruised arm and a bad gash on the forehead.
4. ______________________ Mr. Warner did not feel completely satisfied in his job as program director of Channel 12.
5. ______________________ The winners of the student council election had not yet been officially announced.

C Complete each sentence with the correct vocabulary word.

sustained **formally** **shrewd** **fulfilled** **exceeded**

1. Lisa and John see each other in the hallway every day, but they have never been ______________________ introduced.
2. The cost of the house repairs ______________________ the Robinsons' budget by several hundred dollars.
3. Is it possible for a woman to be ______________________ as a mother and homemaker?
4. Clifford ______________________ a great loss when his dog, a lovable fox terrier, was killed by a car.
5. After careful research, the bankers made a ______________________ decision to raise interest rates.

Personal Words Follow-up

Use a dictionary to find the definitions for the personal words you chose at the beginning of this lesson. If a word has more than one meaning, look for the meaning that defines the word as it is used in the selection. Then write the words and their dictionary definitions in the Personal Words pages at the back of the book.

12 Word Study

The prefix *ex-*, meaning "out of," "from," or "former," appears in many English words. When it is attached to the names of occupations, it usually means "former," such as in the words *ex-president, ex-baseball star,* and *ex-sailor.* In many words, *ex-* carries its "out of" meaning. The word *exclude,* for example, means "to shut out or keep out." The related word *exclusive* means "not shared with others." The *clu* in *exclude* and *exclusive* comes from the Latin root *clausere* meaning "close" or "shut." The word *closet* comes from a closely related root meaning "enclosure." The Latin word *spirare* means "to breathe" and is the root of *expire,* which means "to come to an end" or "to die."

Another common prefix is *mis-*. It means "the opposite of," "the lack of," "badly," or "wrongly" and generally gives a base word an opposite meaning or a meaning that is negative. For example, *calculate* means "to figure out something." But if you miscalculate, you have figured out something incorrectly. If this happens, you would be suffering from a misconception—a wrong understanding of something.

Word Part	Meaning	English Word
ex-	out of; from; former	ex-president
clu	close; shut out	exclude
mis-	opposite of; the lack of; badly; wrongly	miscalculate

Finding Meanings

Write each word or word part beside its meaning.

mis- **clu** **exclude** **miscalculate** **ex-**

1. to close; shut out ________________
2. former ________________
3. to figure wrongly ________________
4. not shared with others ________________
5. opposite of; the lack of; badly; wrongly ________________

True or False

Write T if a statement is true or F if it is false.

__________ 1. Reporters from many newspapers or television stations participate in an exclusive interview.

__________ 2. People who believed that the earth was flat had a misconception about the structure of the planet.

__________ 3. A misinterpretation is a total understanding of an idea or theory.

__________ 4. An ex-pilot no longer commands an aircraft.

__________ 5. To add 2 plus 2 and come up with 5 is to miscalculate.

Choose an Answer

Put an **X** beside the correct answer.

1. When you breathe, you inhale, then
   - ☐ a. expire.
   - ☐ b. exhale.
   - ☐ c. exclude.

2. To behave badly is to
   - ☐ a. misbehave.
   - ☐ b. mistake.
   - ☐ c. mislay.

3. An organization to which only businessmen can belong is
   - ☐ a. expensive.
   - ☐ b. exclusive.
   - ☐ c. objective.

4. A library card that can no longer be used has
   - ☐ a. miscalculated.
   - ☐ b. exhaled.
   - ☐ c. expired.

5. The opposite of *interior* is
   - ☐ a. inside.
   - ☐ b. external.
   - ☐ c. exterior.

9-12 Review and Extension

Multiple Meanings

Some of the vocabulary words you studied in lessons 9 and 11 have more than one meaning. Complete each sentence in this exercise with a vocabulary word from the list below. In these sentences, the words have different meanings than they had in the selection you read. If you are unsure of the various meanings of a word, look it up in the glossary.

fulfilled **conducted** **devote** **sustain** **formally**

1. The architects were asked to design a small bridge that could ________________ the equivalent weight of eight grown elephants.
2. Electricity is normally ________________ by means of wires running from the source of power to the electrical appliance.
3. As best man at his brother's wedding, Jim had to dress ________________ , in a tuxedo.
4. Some people feel such a strong desire to see all the countries of the world working together that they ________________ themselves completely to the cause of world peace.
5. After years of hard work, Alicia finally ________________ her lifelong dream of a travel adventure by setting off on a trip around the world.

Word Parts Review

Complete each sentence so that it makes sense and shows the meaning of the boldfaced vocabulary word.

1. The letter was so **illegible** that ________________________________

____

2. Because Sophie believed in **nonviolence,** she ________________________________

____

3. As an **ex-baseball player** he had more time for ________________________________

____

4. When making potato salad, Jim **excludes** onions because ________________________________

____

5. Since she is **incapable** of getting to the dance, Beth ________________________________

____

6. Because he is **illiterate,** Sam decided to ________________________________

____

7. The tree was **inhabited** by squirrels and ________________________________

____

8. After the tornado the **exterior** of the building was ________________________________

____

9. When CBS got **exclusive** rights to televise the Olympics, ________________________________

____

10. It was **impossible** to keep the children away from the pool because ________________

____

Synonym Study

Following are synonym studies for two vocabulary words you studied in lessons 9 and 11. Use either the vocabulary words or their synonyms to complete the sentences in this exercise. Refer to the synonym studies as you decide which choice carries the best meaning for the specific context of each sentence.

discontinue **pause**

Discontinue and *pause* both mean "to stop an action." Discontinue, however, is used when speaking of the permanent stopping of a regular activity or practice. *Tom discontinued his piano lessons because he didn't have enough time to practice. Pause* means "to stop for a short time." *Cindy paused in her walk to pick some flowers.*

1. Carol decided to ________________________ her subscription to the news magazine.

2. When there was a ________________________ in the conversation, Danny told his joke.

intelligent **shrewd** **clever**

Intelligent, shrewd, and *clever* all mean "mentally sharp or quick." *Intelligent* is usually used when speaking of someone's ability to do well in new situations or to solve problems. *It is clear from the fact that Robert can look at any machine and figure out how it works that he is very intelligent.* Clever suggests a natural quickness or skill in doing a particular thing. *Roger is very clever at making up puns.* Shrewd suggests cleverness and craftiness in practical things. It often implies mischievousness and meanness. *Max shrewdly asked for more money than the car was worth, knowing that customers like to bargain.*

3. It is obvious from the way Mindy talks other people into doing her work for her that

   she is quite ________________________

4. Tony is very ________________________ when it comes to writing vocabulary sentences in class.

5. Frieda was ________________________ enough to teach herself computer programming.

Word Forms

The words listed below are other forms of the vocabulary words you worked with in lessons 9 and 11. Fill in the blank in each sentence with the appropriate word. If you are unsure of the meaning of a word, look it up in the glossary.

formalized **conductor** **excess**

devotion **fulfillment** **sustenance**

1. So many people volunteered to clean up the neighborhood that there was actually an

   ________________________ of help for the project.

2. Pablo's mother packed a lunch of peanut butter sandwiches and fruit for

   ________________________ on the long train trip.

3. In January Ted and Mary Jane decided to marry, but their engagement was not

   ________________________ until early March.

4. For Andrea, becoming a doctor was the ________________________ of a lifelong dream.

5. A solar panel serves as a ________________________ of heat and energy from the sun.

6. In Asia, ________________________ to one's elders is an important element of family life.

Using Your Vocabulary

This word-search puzzle contains 15 vocabulary words from lessons 5–12. They are printed horizontally, vertically, diagonally, backward, and upside down. Begin by writing the vocabulary words on a separate sheet of paper. Then find the words in the puzzle, circling them as you locate them.

1. cure
2. put an end to an activity
3. against the law
4. imprisoned
5. having no manners; uncultured
6. body position
7. serious, harsh
8. the giving of great care and attention to something
9. to shut or keep out
10. to calculate incorrectly
11. not for purposes of making money
12. lively and spirited
13. next to
14. not capable
15. performed; carried out

b	c	e	i	v	b	a	u	n	c	i	v	i	l	i	z	e	d	t	b	d
i	p	h	l	n	n	e	o	c	o	i	o	a	d	v	b	i	i	c	w	o
e	f	i	v	o	g	p	d	e	n	a	d	e	b	c	i	p	q	l	e	u
g	e	o	c	i	t	g	s	r	d	q	e	i	i	o	b	i	x	o	b	p
e	r	o	p	b	m	m	n	e	u	n	i	t	n	o	c	s	i	d	o	w
g	i	v	o	b	m	d	g	s	c	o	e	g	i	a	s	i	p	o	s	t
h	f	r	w	p	i	o	r	e	t	i	o	p	g	h	k	o	i	p	s	e
t	r	e	i	p	h	l	g	m	e	t	r	e	s	r	t	p	r	g	h	l
r	o	n	o	i	t	o	v	e	d	d	r	i	o	p	i	i	o	p	r	t
p	o	o	i	l	p	o	v	e	d	o	i	w	a	g	g	d	g	p	e	n
t	r	n	o	e	a	i	o	n	m	g	e	o	i	h	e	t	r	l	p	t
w	r	p	o	i	o	g	i	e	g	o	h	v	t	o	i	e	b	o	p	b
o	t	r	i	o	n	g	e	i	e	g	v	l	e	r	t	a	p	m	l	n
t	y	o	a	s	f	x	i	l	o	t	y	r	d	p	p	e	r	i	u	l
e	t	f	o	j	c	o	l	g	l	y	r	t	a	a	w	y	r	s	h	d
d	t	i	p	l	s	d	v	j	k	i	y	g	c	n	b	c	r	c	k	h
h	g	t	u	e	d	s	u	p	l	g	m	n	d	s	g	v	n	a	g	r
f	t	d	h	b	n	p	l	m	h	u	i	a	e	s	d	c	g	l	g	e
s	e	v	b	o	p	l	m	s	t	e	r	n	i	n	g	e	d	c	o	m
w	r	d	t	h	g	p	l	u	m	n	v	g	d	t	e	r	s	u	t	e
a	s	d	r	w	h	g	u	p	l	m	f	n	h	t	y	e	d	l	t	d
p	d	e	n	i	f	n	o	c	i	t	d	a	v	b	p	k	l	a	r	y
w	r	t	p	l	h	m	f	t	e	v	d	t	r	w	p	l	g	t	t	v
h	b	t	d	r	e	w	p	l	n	j	w	r	t	b	d	v	p	e	y	h
e	t	g	d	b	v	c	p	l	a	y	o	p	o	s	t	u	r	e	h	g
d	c	u	p	l	h	m	b	c	y	p	k	g	j	b	u	t	r	s	r	w
a	r	t	p	l	g	m	e	w	t	e	h	b	n	f	m	p	l	e	r	w
p	l	h	m	r	t	n	e	t	h	m	f	b	c	e	p	l	y	r	n	d
a	r	c	e	y	t	n	e	b	v	g	t	p	l	u	h	m	t	r	e	w

Word Play

Fictionary

What is the meaning of this? That's the question that forms the basis of the game of Fictionary. There is no need to be a whiz at words to enjoy the game. The main requirements are imagination and a sense of humor. You'll also need a dictionary, some pencils and paper, and at least three people (but the more the better!).

In Fictionary, you are asked to make up definitions for words that you don't know the real meaning of. The definitions should sound as much like real dictionary definitions as possible, because the object of the game is to fool the other players into believing that your definition is the true one—that's where the "fiction" part of the game's name comes from. The fictitious definitions can get pretty absurd, and sometimes hilarious, but then some of the real definitions turn out to be awfully strange too.

Intrigued? Here are the rules:

1. Give each person several slips of paper or index cards and a pen or pencil. Have players write their names on their cards. Each person plays for himself or herself—there are no teams.
2. Choose a leader for the first round. (After the first round, each person in the group should take a turn being the leader.) The leader picks a word that no one knows the meaning of from the dictionary. If any player knows the word, he or she must say so, and a different word should be picked. The leader says the word and spells it for the other players.
3. Every player, including the leader, writes a definition for the word. The leader writes the real definition. Other players try to write as clever and real-sounding a definition as they can.
4. When everyone has written a definition, the leader collects the cards and numbers them. The numbers are used instead of the players' names to identify the definitions. That way no one knows who wrote which definition. The leader reads all the definitions out loud, including the real definition, identifying each by number.
5. Every player votes out loud, by number, for the definition he or she thinks is correct. The leader tallies the votes for each definition.
6. Points are scored in two ways. First, anyone who votes for the correct definition gets a point. Second, a player gets a point for each vote his or her definition collects.

Play continues until time runs out or until a set number of points is reached. The player with the most points wins.

*"**paprika** noun. a small fur-bearing animal having unusually long claws, known for its high altitude nesting."*

13 Where Lincoln Lived

For the first 35 years of his life, Abraham Lincoln seemed to be always on the move. A log-cabin boy and frontiersman, he later wrote of himself as "a piece of floating driftwood." His boyhood homes were scattered across several states: Kentucky, Indiana, and Illinois. At 21 he became a clerk at a store in New Salem, Illinois, at night stretching out his large frame on piles of straw in the back room. Even after he started practicing law he had no **fixed** home, but followed his cases from one small town to another.

When Springfield was named the state capital of Illinois, Lincoln thought the time had come to settle down. He rode into Springfield on a borrowed horse, with all his personal **effects** on his back and in his saddlebags.

Lincoln married Mary Todd in 1842. The first years of their life together were spent in boarding houses and at the Globe Tavern. After the birth of their son Robert, they bought a house on the corner of Eighth and Jackson Streets. The only home Lincoln ever owned cost a **mere** $1,500. He and his family lived there until he was elected president in 1861.

Lincoln had planned to go back to Springfield and to the house at Eighth and Jackson when his term in Washington was up. The presidency, he always said, was only an **interlude.** So he rented the house to a friend and told Billy Herndon, his law partner, to leave their office sign untouched. "If I live, I'm coming back, and we'll go right on practicing law as if nothing ever happened." But Lincoln never did return, for he was assassinated while in office.

Lincoln's Springfield home has been **restored.** Visitors can view the parlor with its plush-covered chairs and floral rugs. They can stand awhile by the four-poster bed in which Lincoln rested after straining his eyes over legal papers in flickering lamplight. They can wander through the sitting room where Mary sewed and Lincoln rocked with young son Tad on his knee. The true heart of Lincoln's memory beats in this simple house.

Personal Words

Choose two words from the selection that are unfamiliar to you or whose meanings you are not completely sure of. (Do not choose words that appear in boldfaced type.) Write the words on the lines provided. Beside each word write what you think it means, based on how it was used in the selection.

1. ______________________ : ____

____

2. ______________________ : ____

____

Using Context

Put an **X** in the box beside each correct answer. For clues to the meanings of the words, reread the parts of the passage in which they appear.

1. In the passage, a **fixed** home is one that
   - ☐ a. is in good repair.
   - ☐ b. is always in the same place.
   - ☐ c. has been decorated by someone else.
   - ☐ d. costs a lot of money.

2. In the passage, Lincoln's **effects** refer to his
   - ☐ a. habits.
   - ☐ b. riding gear.
   - ☐ c. belongings.
   - ☐ d. attitudes.

3. A **mere** $1,500 means
   - ☐ a. only that small amount.
   - ☐ b. approximately $1,500.
   - ☐ c. an enormous sum.
   - ☐ d. stolen money.

4. A **restored** home is one that has been
   - ☐ a. modernized.
   - ☐ b. returned to its original condition.
   - ☐ c. made into a store.
   - ☐ d. rebuilt for storage.

5. When Lincoln said the presidency was only an **interlude,** he meant that it
   - ☐ a. was just a job.
   - ☐ b. didn't pay enough for him to live on.
   - ☐ c. took him too far from his home.
   - ☐ d. was a temporary break from his lifework as a lawyer.

Making Connections

A Write each vocabulary word in front of its definition as it is used in the selection.

fixed **effects** **mere** **restored** **interlude**

1. ______________________ no more than specified; only
2. ______________________ stationary; remaining in one place
3. ______________________ a short period in between
4. ______________________ repaired; returned to its original condition
5. ______________________ personal property; belongings

B On the line next to each word or phrase, write the vocabulary word that is related to it. The related word may be a synonym, an antonym, or a definition for the vocabulary word.

fixed **effects** **mere** **restored** **interlude**

1. simple ____________________
2. stationary ____________________
3. destroyed ____________________
4. main event ____________________
5. tremendous ____________________
6. personal property ____________________
7. small ____________________
8. time in between ____________________
9. space ____________________
10. bare ____________________
11. belongings ____________________
12. unchanging ____________________
13. movable ____________________
14. fixed up ____________________

C Complete each sentence with the correct vocabulary word.

fixed **effects** **mere** **restored** **interlude**

1. Jose was please to see so many old buildings in his neighborhood ____________________ to bring out their 19th-century charm.
2. The statue was ____________________ on its base.
3. Sarah, a ____________________ country girl, had a hard time adjusting to the sophistication of her new city friends.
4. After a brief ____________________ of light-hearted joking, the mayor returned to the serious business at hand.
5. The crash victims' families were given their relatives' ____________________

Personal Words Follow-up

Use a dictionary to find the definitions for the personal words you chose at the beginning of this lesson. If a word has more than one meaning, look for the meaning that defines the word as it is used in the selection. Then write the words and their dictionary definitions in the Personal Words pages at the back of the book.

14 Word Study

The prefix *over-* is one that you most likely use all the time. It appears at the beginning of such common words as *overhead, oversleep,* and *overnight.* If you think about these words, you can probably figure out that *over-* means "above," "across," "too much," or "extra," depending on the root or base word to which it is added. For example, an oversight is an error made by accidentally leaving out, or overlooking, something. Something that is overlooked, of course, is not noticed. *Overstate* means "to support too strongly," while *overwhelm* means "to be overcome by strong feelings, either good or bad." From studying the prefix *over-,* you can figure out that *overdress* means "to dress too warmly" or "to dress too well for an occasion."

Another prefix that is found in many words is *extra-,* meaning "beyond" or "outside." If something is extraordinary, it is beyond or above the usual or ordinary. You may participate in an extracurricular activity, such as soccer. *Extracurricular* means "not part of the regular course of study" or "outside the school day." When a statement is extraneous, it is outside the discussion and has nothing to do with the subject. Someone who is extravagant does things lavishly or beyond reasonable limits.

Word Part	Meaning	English Word
over-	above; across; too much; extra	oversight, overlooked
extra-	beyond; outside	extraordinary, extracurricular

Finding Meanings

Write each word or word part beside its meaning.

over- **oversight** **extraordinary** **overwhelm** **extra-**

1. a mistake ________________
2. to overcome by strong feelings ________________
3. beyond; outside ________________
4. beyond the usual ________________
5. above; across; too much; extra ________________

True or False

Write T if a statement is true or F it is false.

________ 1. To overwhelm someone with your presence is to make her feel comfortable, even bored.

________ 2. Math is an extracurricular activity at school.

________ 3. If you are overdressed, you are wearing clothes too fancy for the occasion.

________ 4. Since she saves her money and rarely buys anything new, she is extravagant.

________ 5. An oversight is a mistake, usually made by accidentally leaving something out.

Answering Questions

1. Which word describes someone who graduates at the top of his class, is an outstanding musician, and a medal-winning athlete? ________________________________

____

2. When or where might you wear an overcoat? ________________________________

____

3. If you did not do well on a paper and the teacher comments that you have too much extraneous information, what does he mean? ________________________________

____

4. Would an extravagant person buy a house or a mansion? ________________________________

____

5. Which word best describes how you would feel if one of your teachers assigned you to read three chapters in your social studies textbook in one night? ________________________________

____

15 America's 16th President

The Lincoln cent was first **issued** in 1909, to celebrate the 100th anniversary of the birth of Abraham Lincoln, 16th president of the United States. One side of the coin bears the profile of Lincoln as he looked during the **trying** years of the War Between the States. At that time, faced with the great problems of a divided nation, Lincoln worked hard to prevent the split between North and South. "A house divided against itself cannot stand," he warned the nation.

From 1909 through 1958, the reverse side of the Lincoln cent had a simple design of two wheat heads (tops of the stalks, which hold the kernels). Wheat stands for **abundance,** which America offers its people not only in material wealth but also in the freedoms and liberties granted by the Constitution.

In 1959, to celebrate the 150th anniversary of Lincoln's birth, a new design was **adopted** for the back of the penny. Created by mint engraver Frank Gasparro, the design featured the Lincoln Memorial in Washington, D.C. Since the memorial is an outstanding tribute to the late president, it was a good choice.

Two years after Lincoln's death, plans were begun to build a monument to honor him. It was finally decided that a fitting memorial would be erected in the nation's capital, at the end of a long mall. Inside the building, a huge statue of Lincoln sitting in a chair symbolizes the greatness of the former president.

Lincoln was a man of **humble** birth. He was born in a log cabin in Kentucky, and as a boy he studied his lessons by candlelight. He enjoyed few of life's material comforts. Yet, through hard work, he rose to become the president of our nation at one of the most difficult times in its history.

Personal Words

Choose two words from the selection that are unfamiliar to you or whose meanings you are not completely sure of. (Do not choose words that appear in boldfaced type.) Write the words on the lines provided. Beside each word write what you think it means, based on how it was used in the selection.

1. ________________________ : ____

____

2. ________________________ : ____

____

Using Context

Circle the correct meaning for each vocabulary word. Then use the word in a sentence of your own.

1. **issued** given away taken spent put into circulation

____

2. **trying** violent suitable unusual difficult

____

3. **humble** modest noble foreign significant

____

4. **abundance** freedom packages opportunity plenty

____

5. **adopted** copies accepted celebrated presented

____

Making Connections

A For each boldfaced vocabulary word in the following sentences, choose a synonym and an antonym from the list that follows. Write the synonyms and antonyms in the blanks.

modest	**distributed**	**easy**	**rejected**	**plentifulness**
difficult	**lack**	**assumed**	**kept**	**boastful**

1. Work began on the uniforms in late January, but they were not **issued** until summer.

   Synonym: ____________________ Antonym: ____________________

2. The months during Jack's illness were **trying** ones for his family.

   Synonym: ____________________ Antonym: ____________________

3. A **humble** woman, Mrs. Rodriguez did not talk about the patience and imagination she employed in her work with handicapped children.

   Synonym: ____________________ Antonym: ____________________

4. There was an **abundance** of food at the school party.

   Synonym: ______________________ Antonym: ______________________

5. The Wongs **adopted** a family policy of eating dinner together.

   Synonym: ______________________ Antonym: ______________________

B Write each vocabulary word on the line in front of the appropriate synonym and antonym.

issued **trying** **humble** **abundance** **adopted**

	Synonym	**Antonym**
1. ______________________	simple	grand
2. ______________________	accepted	rejected
3. ______________________	circulated	collected
4. ______________________	taxing	easy
5. ______________________	plenty	scarcity

C Complete the following analogies by inserting one of the five vocabulary words in the blank at the end of each one. Remember that in an analogy the last two words or phrases must be related to each other in the same way that the first two are related.

issued **trying** **humble** **abundance** **adopted**

1. George Washington : honest : : Abraham Lincoln : ______________________
2. full : overflowing : : excess : ______________________
3. book : published : : coin : ______________________
4. acquired : ought : : taken on : ______________________
5. valuable : worthless : : effortless : ______________________

Personal Words Follow-up

Use a dictionary to find the definitions for the personal words you chose at the beginning of this lesson. If a word has more than one meaning, look for the meaning that defines the word as it is used in the selection. Then write the words and their dictionary definitions in the Personal Words pages at the back of the book.

16 Word Study

The prefix *re-* is one of the most common in the English language. It comes from a Latin word meaning "back" or "again." *Re-* appears in dozens of words you already know. *Repay,* for instance, means "to pay back," and *redo* means "to do again." *Reply* means "to answer." A reply, then, is something said back. To recede is to withdraw, or to move back or away. A related word is recess, a time when work stops or a "going back" from work. *Recess* also means "a place in a wall that is set back from the rest of the wall." You might remember from lesson 12 that *clu* means "shut." Therefore, a recluse is a person who chooses to live alone, shut away from society.

Another common word that has the same root as *recede* and *recess* is *proceed,* which means "to go forward." The prefix *pro-* means "forward." A procedure is a set of actions done in a particular order, or a way of accomplishing something. The root *ject* means "to throw" or "to force" and appears in both *reject* and *project. Reject* means "to refuse to accept something," and *project* means "to throw" or "to shoot forward." In the word *protest* the root *test* means "to witness or testify." Therefore, to protest means to testify, or state, that you object to something.

Word Part	Meaning	English Word
re-	back; again	repay, reply, recede, recluse
pro-	forward	proceed
ject	to throw; to force	project, reject
test	to witness; to testify	protest

Finding Meanings

Write each word or word part beside its meaning.

re- **recluse** **test** **ject** **pro-**

1. to throw; to force ____________________
2. forward ____________________
3. someone who chooses to live alone ____________________
4. to witness; to testify ____________________
5. back; again ____________________

True or False

Write T if a statement is true or F if it is false.

__________ 1. A prisoner alone in his cell is a recluse.

__________ 2. A procedure is a set of actions done in a particular order.

__________ 3. A rejected offer is one that is immediately accepted.

__________ 4. A doctor or a nurse will use a needle to give an ejection.

__________ 5. In order to practice for an important test, students sometimes take a protest.

Choose an Answer

Put an **X** in front of the answer choice you think is correct.

1. When Congress stops work for a vacation or holiday, it declares a
   - ☐ a. recluse.
   - ☐ b. recount.
   - ☐ c. recess.
2. At low tide, the water at a beach
   - ☐ a. recedes.
   - ☐ b. recesses.
   - ☐ c. replies.
3. If you enter a drawing contest and your entry is rejected, you
   - ☐ a. win first prize.
   - ☐ b. do not get a prize.
   - ☐ c. can enter again.
4. If you're told to do a job a certain way, you are being asked to follow a
   - ☐ a. procedure.
   - ☐ b. project.
   - ☐ c. protest.
5. To make strong objections to something is to
   - ☐ a. protest.
   - ☐ b. pretest.
   - ☐ c. reject.

13-16 Review and Extension

Multiple Meanings

Some of the vocabulary words you studied in lessons 13 and 15 have more than one meaning. Read each word listed below and its definitions. Next to each sentence that follows, write the letter of the definition that matches the meaning of the word as it is used in that sentence.

fixed

a. (adj.) not movable
b. (adj.) settled; set
c. (v.) repaired

__________ 1. The buoy is anchored in a **fixed** position in the harbor.

__________ 2. That is a **fixed** price; there is no room for bargaining.

__________ 3. After Sally had **fixed** the chain on her bicycle, she was covered with grease.

trying

a. (v.) attempting
b. (adj.) annoying; hard to bear

__________ 4. Because Gary's mother finds the sound of rock music **trying,** she asks Gary to wear headphones when listening to his stereo.

__________ 5. **Trying** too hard at something can lead to frustration.

__________ 6. After a **trying** day, Mr. Conrad likes to sit back and read a good book.

effects

a. (n.) something brought about by a cause; results
b. (v.) to bring about; to cause

__________ 7. Susan's blindness was one of the **effects** of the accident.

__________ 8. We hope the new curfew **effects** a change in the truancy rate at the high school.

__________ 9. That photographer is known for using black and white film to create dramatic **effects.**

Word Parts Review

Complete each sentence so that it makes sense and shows the meaning of the boldfaced vocabulary word.

1. Because of an **oversight,** John's name ______________________________

   ____
2. The **extracurricular** basketball team met after school because _______________

   ____
3. By **overstating** his opinion, Will __________________________________

   ____
4. **Overwhelmed** by the sad news, Martha had to _________________________

   ____
5. Everyone in the class had to **redo** the assignment because __________________

   ____
6. The workers **protested** against the cut in pay by ________________________

   ____
7. Amy felt sad as she watched the boat **recede** because ______________________

   ____
8. Even though he followed the **procedure,** he could not ______________________

   ____
9. The room looked very **extravagant** with its ___________________________

   ____
10. Colin explained that following **procedure** was important because ____________

    ____

Synonym Study

Following are synonym studies for two vocabulary words you studied in lessons 13 and 15. Use either the vocabulary words or their synonyms to complete the sentences in this exercise. Refer to the synonym studies as you decide which choice best fits the context of each sentence.

restore **renew** **repair**

Restore, renew, and *repair* all have to do with fixing things. Restore is used when speaking of working on old buildings and furniture to make them look exactly as they did when they were new. *The Westons restored the run-down farmhouse in the style of the 1850s, when it was built. Renew* means "to make something fresh or complete again." *Janet's confidence was renewed when she got the part she wanted in the play.* To repair is to fix a damaged or broken item. *Jack had to repair the broken window.*

trying **difficult**

Trying and *difficult* both mean "hard to do" or "hard to deal with." *Difficult* means "hard to do, to figure out, to understand, or to accomplish." It implies the need to do something: to overcome an obstacle, to learn something, or to solve a problem. With a difficulty, patience, skill, or courage is usually required. *Hal finds algebra difficult, so he spends more time studying it than he does other subjects. Trying* means "upsetting" or "especially hard to bear or put up with." It also means "annoying." Something that is trying calls for no direct action. It just has to be lived through, put up with, or avoided. *Cindy found her little brother's teasing so trying that she went to her room and closed the door. Helen finds the pressure of her work so trying that she is looking for a less demanding job.*

1. After it was ____________________, the rolltop desk looked just as it had when Celia's grandfather made it.
2. Greg found it ____________________ to listen to Ellen's bad jokes and puns.
3. The brakes on Joshua's bicycle were sticking, so he had to ____________________ them.
4. All Mrs. Lopez needed to ____________________ her energy after her long trip was a hot bath and a good night's sleep.
5. Pat found it ____________________ to build a coop for her rabbits, but she stuck with the project until it was finished and her pets had a new home.

Word Forms

The words below are other forms of the vocabulary words you worked with in lessons 13 and 15. Fill in the blank in each sentence with the appropriate word. If you are unsure of the meaning of a word, refer to the glossary.

adoption	**humility**	**fixedly**
restoration	**merely**	**abundant**

1. The ______________________ of the old train station had hardly begun when a proposal was brought before the city council to build a new one instead.
2. Though the poet was internationally famous, her ______________________ came across in the simple, quiet way in which she spoke.
3. The Russian immigrants were shocked by the ______________________ supply of food available in every grocery store in the United States.
4. Michael sat ______________________ waiting for more than an hour for the results of his history exam.
5. Most of the seventh-graders voted against the ______________________ of a rule outlawing balls on the school grounds.
6. Antonio thought of Maria as a close friend, not ______________________ as a cousin.

Using Your Vocabulary

Use vocabulary words introduced in lessons 9–16 to solve the word puzzle on page 64. For each definition or synonym, think of a vocabulary word that has the same meaning. Write the word in the puzzle space beside its definition. The number of lines in each answer space and the letter that is given provide clues to the word. Notice that the letters in the circles form a phrase related to Abraham Lincoln. Write the phrase on the line provided.

1. not grand; modest and unassuming _ _ _ _ ◯ _
2. dedicate _ _ _ ◯ _ _
3. difficult or wearing _ _ _ _ _ ◯
4. belongings _ _ _ _ ◯ _ _
5. make up for a debt _ _ _ ◯ _
6. plentifulness _ ◯ _ _ _ _ _ _ _
7. underwent _ _ _ _ _ ◯ _ _ _
8. lived in _ ◯ _ _ _ _ _ _ _
9. incorrect; not proper _ _ ◯ _ _ _ _ _
10. come to an end _ _ _ _ ◯ _
11. withdraw or move back _ _ _ _ _ ◯
12. work or study break _ _ _ _ ◯ _
13. stationary _ ◯ _ _ _
14. dress too warmly _ _ _ _ ◯ _ _ _ _
15. put into circulation _ _ _ _ ◯
16. a conclusion reached through reasoning _ _ _ _ _ _ _ _ ◯
17. brief period in between _ _ ◯ _ _ _ _ _ _

Phrase: ____________________

17 The Birth of Basketball

Unlike most sports, which evolved over time from street games, basketball was designed by one man to suit a particular purpose. The man was Dr. James Naismith, and his purpose was to invent a **vigorous** game that could be played indoors during the winter.

In 1891, Naismith was an instructor at the International YMCA Training School, now Springfield College, in Massachusetts. The school trained physical education instructors for YMCAs throughout the country. That year the school was trying to come up with a physical activity that the men could enjoy between the football and baseball seasons. None of the standard indoor activities held their interest for long. Naismith was asked to solve the problem.

He first tried to adapt some of the popular outdoor sports, but they were all too rough. The men were getting bruised from tackling each other and being hit with equipment. Windows were getting smashed.

Finally Naismith decided to try to invent a game that would **incorporate** the most common elements of outdoor team sports without the physical contact. He noted that most of the popular sports used a ball. He chose a soccer ball, because it was soft and large enough that it required no equipment, such as a bat or a racket, to **propel** it. That ensured that the ball wouldn't travel too fast. Next he decided on an elevated goal, so that scoring would depend on skill and accuracy rather than on brute strength. His goals were two peach baskets, **affixed** to 10-foot-high balconies at each end of the gym. Naismith then wrote 13 rules **delineating** the specifics of the game. Many of those rules are still in effect.

Basketball was an immediate success. The students taught it to their friends, and the new sport quickly caught on. People have been dribbling ever since.

Personal Words

Choose two words from the selection that are unfamiliar to you or whose meanings you are not completely sure of. (Do not choose words that appear in boldfaced type.) Write the words on the lines provided. Beside each word write what you think it means, based on how it was used in the selection.

1. ______________________ : ____

____

2. ______________________ : ____

____

Using Context

Put an **X** in the box beside the best definition for each boldfaced word. For clues to the meanings of words, reread the parts of the passage in which they appear.

1. The man was Dr. James Naismith, and his purpose was to invent a **vigorous** game that could be played indoors during the winter.
   - ☐ a. physically active and energetic
   - ☐ b. complex
   - ☐ c. violent
   - ☐ d. slow and easygoing
2. His goals were two peach baskets, **affixed** to 10-foot-high balconies at each end of the gym.
   - ☐ a. fastened securely
   - ☐ b. painted onto
   - ☐ c. built into
   - ☐ d. draped loosely over
3. Naismith then wrote 13 rules **delineating** the specifics of the game.
   - ☐ a. lining up side by side
   - ☐ b. describing in detail
   - ☐ c. examining
   - ☐ d. researching
4. Finally Naismith decided to try to invent a game that would **incorporate** the most common elements of outdoor team sports without the physical contact.
   - ☐ a. leave out of the game
   - ☐ b. define
   - ☐ c. change around
   - ☐ d. work into the game
5. He chose a soccer ball, because it was soft and large enough that it required no equipment, such as a bat or a racket, to **propel** it.
   - ☐ a. hit it properly
   - ☐ b. break it apart
   - ☐ c. drive it forward
   - ☐ d. hold it tightly

Making Connections

A Write each vocabulary word on the line in front of the appropriate synonym and antonym.

vigorous **incorporate** **propel** **affix** **delineate**

		Synonym	Antonym
1.	______________________	attach	remove
2.	______________________	energetic	slow-moving
3.	______________________	include	eliminate
4.	______________________	push	pull
5.	______________________	specify	generalize

B Complete the following analogies by inserting one of the five vocabulary words in the blank at the end of each one. Remember that in an analogy the last two words or phrases must be related in the same way that the first two are related.

vigorous **incorporating** **propel** **affixed** **delineate**

1. clasp : hold : : push : ______________________
2. questions : inquire : : definitions : ______________________
3. boring : dull : : energetic : ______________________
4. increasing : enlarging : :including : ______________________
5. dug : filled in : : removed : ______________________

C Complete each sentence with the correct vocabulary word.

vigorous **incorporate** **propel** **affixed** **delineate**

1. Jeannie crouched at the starting line, ready to ______________________ herself forward the moment she heard the gun.
2. As supervisor of the group, Hank was assigned to ______________________ the procedure that was to be followed in carrying out the operation.
3. Mr. Wilcox decided to ______________________ a touch of elegance into his homey, unpretentious restaurant.
4. ______________________ to the bumper of the car in front of Mariel was a sticker that read, "If you can read this, you're too close."
5. The stain that Violet was using on her bookcase would not come off her hands without a ______________________ scrubbing.

Personal Words Follow-up

Use a dictionary to find the definitions for the personal words you chose at the beginning of this lesson. If a word has more than one meaning, look for the meaning that defines the word as it is used in the selection. Then write the words and their dictionary definitions in the Personal Words pages at the back of the book. How close did you come to figuring out their meanings for yourself?

18 Word Study

You probably know that *transport* means "to carry something from one place to another." The word part *trans-* means "across" or "beyond," and the root *port* means "to carry." A porter is a person who carries things for other people. The root *port* also means "harbor" or "gate." The place in which ships anchor may be called either a harbor or a port. The places where airplanes land and are kept is, of course, called an airport. Likewise, space vehicles are kept in spaceports, and automobiles in carports.

It is from ports of various kinds that goods are exported and imported—sent out and taken in. The prefix *ex-*, from Lesson 12, means "out of" or "from," and the prefix *im-,* from Lesson 10, means "in."

Transfer has a meaning that is similar to the meaning of *transport.* The root *fer* means "to carry" or "to bear." Both transport and transfer refer to moving things, but transport refers to the action of actually carrying something somewhere, while transfer refers to the changing of location without mention of the actual carrying.

Word Part	Meaning	English Word
trans-	across; beyond	transport, transfer
port	to carry; harbor; gate	transport, porter, port
ex-	out of; from	export
im-	in	import
fer	to carry; to bear	transfer

Finding Meanings

Write each word or word part beside its meaning.

trans- **port** **ex-** **im-** **transfer**

1. carrying something from one place to another ____________
2. out of; from ____________
3. in ____________
4. harbor ____________
5. across; beyond ____________

True or False

Write T if a statement is true of F if it is false.

__________ 1. A landing and taking off place for a helicopter is called a heliport.

__________ 2. A policewoman who is sent from one precinct to another across town has been given a transfer.

__________ 3. An import is something that cannot be brought in from another place.

__________ 4. When a person sells a house, he turns over the deed to the new owner. In other words, the two people transport the deed.

__________ 5. When the United States takes in coffee beans from South America, the United States imports those beans.

Choose an Answer

Put an **X** in the box beside the correct answer.

1. A radio message that is sent across the ocean from England to America could be called
   - ☐ a. transatlantic.
   - ☐ b. transported.
   - ☐ c. exported.

2. A building that explodes sends particles hurtling out, so a building that collapses in on itself, sending particles inward, is said to
   - ☐ a. deplode.
   - ☐ b. implode.
   - ☐ c. unplode.

3. Since *port* means "to carry" and *-able* means "capable of," it stands to reason that *portable* means "capable of
   - ☐ a. standing still."
   - ☐ b. being carried."
   - ☐ c. generating power."

4. If we know *re-* means "back" or "again," then newspaper people who observe events, write about those events, and send what they've written back to their papers are called
   - ☐ a. readers.
   - ☐ b. recorders.
   - ☐ c. reporters.

5. Coffee is a Colombian
   - ☐ a. transfer.
   - ☐ b. transport.
   - ☐ c. export.

19 In-Line Skating

You might call them Rollerblades—many people do—since most people believe that the sport began with the invention of the Rollerblade in 1980. This is and isn't true. The Rollerblade company did make the in-line skate practical and popular, and it still sells more in-line skates than anybody else. But did you know that the in-line skate was really invented over 300 years ago, in Holland?

In order to understand how this could be, you need to know more about what an in-line skate is. Like the once popular roller skate, it's a boot with wheels. But, unlike a roller skate, an in-line skate has wheels that are all in a straight row. Modern in-line skates have anywhere from three to five wheels. The straight-line **configuration** of the wheels is what gives in-line skates their speed and **maneuverability,** and what makes them a special favorite with ice skaters, because they feel so much like ice skates when you're on them.

In fact, that's exactly what **prompted** the invention of in-line skates. A Dutch inventor wanted to enjoy the feeling of ice skates even in summer, so he attached wooden spools to his shoes, and away he went. Various others came up with similar designs throughout the 18th century.

Over a century later, an American, James Plimpton, invented the roller skate. His design gained instant popularity, featuring two sets of two side-by-side wheels. But while roller skates became popular, they didn't offer anything close to the **sensation** ice skaters wanted.

It took two brothers from Minneapolis, Scott and Brennan Olson, to come up with that feeling. Using an old Dutch skate as a model, they came up with the first modern in-line skate. They called it the "Rollerblade" and started selling it in 1980. As with skateboards, the **advent** of comfortable high-quality urethane wheels made possible new levels of performance.

Personal Words

Choose two words from the selection that are unfamiliar to you or whose meanings you are not completely sure of. (Do not choose words that appear in boldfaced type.) Write the words on the lines provided. Beside each word write what you think it means, based on how it was used in the selection.

1. ______________________ : ____

____

2. ______________________ : ____

____

Using Context

Put an **X** in the box beside each correct answer. For clues to the meanings of the words, reread the parts of the passage in which they appear.

1. The **configuration** of rollerskate wheels refers to the wheels'
   - ☐ a. motion.
   - ☐ b. size.
   - ☐ c. shape.
   - ☐ d. speed.

2. The **sensation** ice-skaters wanted was something that
   - ☐ a. created a feeling.
   - ☐ b. is new and different.
   - ☐ c. can be touched.
   - ☐ d. was popular.

3. To say the invention was **prompted** means that it was
   - ☐ a. caused to happen.
   - ☐ b. forced to happen.
   - ☐ c. stopped from happening.
   - ☐ d. just beginning.

4. If the wheels on in-line skates give them speed and maneuverability, we can infer that **maneuverability** must describe something that
   - ☐ a. does not bend or change.
   - ☐ b. is easy to do.
   - ☐ c. moves easily.
   - ☐ d. moves quickly.

5. In the clause "the **advent** of comfortable high-quality urethane wheels made possible new levels of performance," *advent* means
   - ☐ a. discovery.
   - ☐ b. popularity.
   - ☐ c. arrival.
   - ☐ d. invention.

Making Connections

A For each vocabulary word, choose a synonym and an antonym from the following list. Write the synonyms and antonyms on the lines provided.

immovability	**inspired**	**clutter**	**feeling**	**departure**
flexibility	**dullness**	**hindered**	**shape**	**arrival**

	Synonym	Antonym
1. **configuration**	____________	____________
2. **maneuverability**	____________	____________
3. **prompted**	____________	____________
4. **sensation**	____________	____________
5. **advent**	____________	____________

B Complete the following analogies by inserting one of the five vocabulary words in the blank at the end of each one. Remember that in an analogy the last two words or phrases must be related in the same way that the first two are related.

configuration **maneuverability** **prompted** **sensation** **advent**

1. awkward : graceful : : stopped : ______________________
2. created : destroyed : : departure : ______________________
3. anger : emotion : : thrill : ______________________
4. pieces : puzzle : : parts : ______________________
5. people : sensibility : : bicycles : ______________________

C Complete each sentence with the correct vocabulary word.

configuration **maneuverability** **prompted** **sensation** **advent**

1. The ______________________ of Sally's 16th birthday meant she would soon get her driver's license.
2. The Internet has ______________________ new ways of getting information.
3. Because of its ______________________ , the race car handled the mountain roads very well.
4. The building's unusual ______________________ made it a well-known skyscraper in the city.
5. Some say the ______________________ one feels while snowboarding is very different from what one feels when snow skiing.

Personal Words Follow-up

Use a dictionary to find the definitions for the personal words you chose at the beginning of this lesson. If a word has more than one meaning, look for the meaning that defines the word as it is used in the selection. Then write the words and their dictionary definitions in the Personal Words pages at the back of the book. How close did you come to figuring out their meanings for yourself?

20 Word Study

When a word has something to do with a number, it frequently includes a prefix from Latin or Greek. The prefixes *semi-, demi-,* and *hemi-* all mean "half" or "partly." The word *semicircle* means "half a circle," *semiofficial* means "partly official," and *semiannual* means "twice a year." The word *demigod* refers to a mythological being with more power than a mortal but less power than a god. The word *hemisphere* means "one-half of the earth," and *hemicycle* means "a curved or semicircular structure." Of the three prefixes, *semi-* occurs most often.

Multi- is another word part that is found in many words and that also involves numbers. When *multi-* precedes a root or base word, it means "more than one or two; many." A multicolored fish has many colors, while a multimillionaire has several million dollars.

Word Part	Meaning	English Word
semi-, demi-, hemi-	half; partly	semicircle demigod, hemisphere
multi-	more than one or two; many	multicolored, multimillionaire

Finding Meanings

Write each word or word part beside its meaning.

hemisphere **multi-** **demi-** **multicolored** **semicircle**

1. having many colors ______________________
2. half of the earth ______________________
3. half a circle ______________________
4. half; partly ______________________
5. many ______________________

True or False

Write T if a statement is true or F if it is false.

__________ 1. A semimonthly club meets two times a month.

__________ 2. Multiplication is the process of adding a number to itself one time.

__________ 3. If a person is considered a demigod, he or she seems almost godlike.

__________ 4. A hemisphere is one-half of the earth.

__________ 5. If you were a multimillionaire, you could easily afford to buy a sports car.

Answering Questions

1. If diamonds are considered precious stones, what do you think semiprecious stones would be?

   ____

2. *Demi-*, means "half," and *tasse* means "cup." What would you expect to get if you ordered a demitasse in a coffee shop? ______________________________

   ____

3. What punctuation mark could you use to show a strong relationship between two independent clauses in a sentence? ______________________________

   ____

4. When there are more than one or two babies born at a time, what are they called? _______

   ____

5. What kinds of stories would you expect to find in a multicultural anthology? __________

   ____

17-20 Review and Extension

Multiple Meanings

Some of the vocabulary words you studied in lessons 17 and 19 have more than one meaning. Read each word listed below and its definitions. Complete each sentence that follows with the correct vocabulary word.

prompted

a. (v.) moved to action
b. (v.) inspired
c. (v.) supplied a performer or speaker with words he or she has forgotten

incorporate

a. (v.) to work something in
b. (v.) to form into a legal corporation

delineate

a. (v.) to describe or set forth in detail
b. (v.) to indicate or mark the outline of

1. The police asked the Block Association to ______________________ their plans for a neighborhood crime-watch network.

2. The odd feeling that something was wrong ______________________ me to return home.

3. Mrs. Rodriguez planted a row of small rosebushes to ______________________ the property line between the two houses.

4. Paula and her partner, Diane, had no idea of the amount of work it would take to ______________________ their small-crafts business.

5. The actor could not continue his lines until he was ______________________ by the director backstage.

6. Nina tried hard to ______________________ her ballet teacher's suggestions into her stage performance.

7. The graffiti in the school ______________________ a school-wide investigation.

8. Theodore used a red felt-tip marker to ______________________ the pre–Civil War borders on his map.

9. Brown and Manor filed all the papers necessary to ______________________ their new law firm.

10. The dark sky and thick clouds ______________________ Matt to head for shelter.

Word Parts Review

Complete each sentence so that it makes sense and shows the meaning of the boldfaced vocabulary word.

1. To **transport** the heavy cannon, the soldiers ______________________
____
2. The country **imports** most of its food because ______________________
____
3. During Jon's **semimonthly** trips to the nursing home he ______________________
____
4. Before she could **transfer** the contents of her locker, ______________________
____
5. The **multicolored** wallpaper made the room look ______________________
____
6. It was interesting to study **demigods** because they ______________________
____
7. Wool is an important **import** for Australia, since ______________________
____
8. The equator divides the earth into northern and southern **hemispheres,** which means
____
9. She drew the moon in the shape of a **semicircle** so that it would look ______________________
____
10. The **multimillionaire** did not hesitate to buy ______________________
____

Synonym Study

Following are synonym studies for three vocabulary words you studied in lessons 17 and 19. Use either the vocabulary words or their synonyms to complete the sentences in this exercise. Refer to the synonym studies as you decide which choice best fits the context of each sentence.

vigorous **strenuous**

Vigorous and *strenuous* mean "having or requiring great vitality or force." Vigorous implies showing no signs of lessening freshness or energy. *A vigorous walk stimulates blood circulation.* Strenuous suggests a difficult or challenging task that tests strength. *An excess of strenuous activity should be avoided by heart patients.*

1. Four hours of lifting proved too ________________________ for Anthony's weak back; he spent the next day and a half in bed with a heating pad.
2. For the final selection, the conductor chose a ________________________ piece of music that would leave the audience in high spirits.
3. The hikers trained long and hard for their ________________________ trek up the mountain.

affix **attach**

Affix and *attach* mean "to make something stay firmly connected to something else." Affix implies directly fixing one object to another, usually permanently, by such means as gluing, stamping, or nailing. *Sidney affixed leather patches to the elbows of her jacket.* Attach suggests joining with the use of a link, tie, bolt, hinge, or other connecting device. *The Joneses attached their camper to their car and set off for a two-week vacation.*

4. Gail used a shoestring to ________________________ her tricycle to her brother's wagon.
5. Applicants were asked to ________________________ a small black-and-white photo of themselves to their application forms using paper clips.
6. After ten hours of driving, Renee did not have the energy even to ________________________ a stamp to an envelope.

propel **push**

Propel and *push* both mean "to force to move forward or aside." Propel suggests driving something quickly forward or onward by any kind of strong force. *The gun propelled the bullet through the air. John propelled the puck across the ice with a swift slice of his hockey stick.* Push implies that the thing providing the force stays in steady contact with the object being moved. In other words, to push is to move by pressing. *Larry braced his hands against the piano and pushed the instrument across the room.*

7. When his car stalled and wouldn't start again, Dave had to get help to

   ______________________ the car to the side of the road.

8. With his strong arm, Bruce could ______________________ a baseball faster than anyone else in the league.

9. To ______________________ the soccer ball across the field, Lucy gave it a powerful kick.

Word Forms

Each sentence below requires you to use a different form of one of the words you studied in lessons 17 and 19. Fill in the blank in each sentence with the appropriate word. If you are unsure of the meaning of a word, look it up in the glossary.

configured	**vigor**	**maneuvered**	**incorporation**	**sensational**
affixing	**delineation**	**propeller**	**promptly**	**invigorating**

1. After Marty carefully ______________________ the model airplane, it still did not match the picture on the box.

2. The Roths planned a little family ceremony for ______________________ the street numbers to their freshly painted house.

3. The sailors returned to their ship with renewed ______________________ after three days of shore liberty.

4. He carefully ______________________ the ship around the icebergs.

5. The Broadway production was the most ______________________ musical that ever hit New York City.

6. Sean wound the ______________________ of his model airplane and let it go.

7. The new design for the train station reflected the ______________________ of the ideas of three architects into one plan.

8. In her interview, Janet asked for a ______________________ of the responsibilities.

9. Gladys and Herbert fantasized about a(n) ______________________ canoe trip down white-water rapids, but they went to Miami instead.

10. When the smoke alarm sounded, we moved ______________________ to the nearest exit.

Using Your Vocabulary

The scrambled words below are all vocabulary words from lessons 13–20. Use the definition or synonym next to each scramble to help you figure out what the word is. Then write the word in the space provided. The number of lines in each answer space also provides a clue to the word. The circled letters will form a phrase related to golf. Write that phrase on the line provided at the bottom of the puzzle.

1. NEVDAT	arrival	_ _ _ _ _ _
2. ITHYMIUL	modesty	○ _ _ _ _ _ _ _
3. EDOAPDT	accepted	_ _ _ _ _ _ _
4. PRNOARSTT	carry	_ _ _ _ _ _ ○ _ _
5. TERCJE	throw back	_ _ _ _ _ _
6. NADEITELI	describe in detail	_ _ ○ _ _ _ _ _ _
7. POMTPR	inspire	_ _ _ _ _ _
8. REEM	only; simple	_ ○ _ _
9. GROVI	energy	_ ○ _ _ _
10. ITMRPO	goods taken in	_ _ _ _ _ _
11. SOETISNAN	feeling	_ _ ○ _ _ _ _ _ _
12. XAFIF	attach	_ _ _ _ _
13. OLERPP	drive forward	_ _ ○ _ _ _
14. FNASRTER	pass on	_ _ _ ○ _ _ _ _
15. DNELRTIU	a short period in between	_ _ _ _ _ _ _ _ _
16. SEDROTER	renewed	_ _ _ _ _ _ _ ○ _

Phrase: ______________________________

21 Debris on Earth

There may not be much you can do to help clean up space **debris,** but you can do something about another serious problem a little closer to home—**marine** debris. Marine debris is trash that is lost in the ocean or dumped or pumped into it. Much of it is plastic—garbage bags, six-pack rings, picnic utensils, foam cups, and resin pellets (the raw form of plastic). Since plastic doesn't break down the way natural products do, this debris may be around for centuries. And since plastic floats, it often ends up littering our beaches or being eaten by birds, turtles, seals, and other sea creatures.

Some marine debris comes from illegal dumping, but most comes from individuals. People still throw trash overboard from their boats, thinking it will sink and cause no harm. Picnickers leave plastic plates, cups, forks, and spoons on the beach, where the tide washes them out to sea. Fishermen dump old fishing lines, nets, and traps into the ocean. Whatever the source, marine debris poses a serious threat to wildlife.

Marine debris is a **hazard** for humans as well as for animals. Fishing lines can get tangled in boat propellers, and plastic bags can clog cooling intakes, causing engine problems or disabling boats. Beaches have had to be closed because medical waste—bottles, syringes, and other items—washes into swimming areas. To eliminate problems like these, we must remove litter from the beaches and reduce the amount of trash that is entering the ocean.

Each year the Center for Marine Conservation in Washington, D.C., holds a National Beach Cleanup on a Saturday in September. In 1998, an **estimated** 200,000 volunteers picked up trash from thousands of miles of coastline in 33 American states and territories and eight foreign countries.

Even if you don't live near the ocean, you can **participate** in helping to reduce the amount of marine debris. After a picnic or boat trip, throw your trash into a garbage can. Never put anything plastic down the toilet. Cut the loops of six-pack rings so animals can't get caught in them. And recycle everything you can. The more each of us does to reduce the amount of trash we produce, the less debris there will be to pollute our water, our air, and our planet.

Personal Words

Choose two words from the selection that are unfamiliar to you or whose meanings you are not completely sure of. (Do not choose words that appear in boldfaced type.) Write the words on the lines provided. Beside each word write what you think it means, based on how it was used in the selection.

1. ____________________ : ____

____

2. ______________________ : ____

____

Using Context

Put an **X** in the box beside the best definition for each boldfaced word. For clues to the meanings of words, reread the parts of the passage in which they appear.

1. There may not be much you can do to help clean up space **debris.**
   - ☐ a. garbage
   - ☐ b. crowding
   - ☐ c. obstacles
   - ☐ d. planets

2. You can do something about another serious problem a little closer to home—**marine** debris.
   - ☐ a. space
   - ☐ b. land
   - ☐ c. sea
   - ☐ d. water

3. Marine debris is a **hazard** for humans.
   - ☐ a. worry
   - ☐ b. source of danger
   - ☐ c. help
   - ☐ d. cause of anger

4. This year, an **estimated** 200,000 volunteers picked up trash from thousands of miles of coastline in 33 American states and territories and 8 foreign countries.
   - ☐ a. concluded
   - ☐ b. counted
   - ☐ c. rounded number
   - ☐ d. judged

5. Schools, scout troops, and other organizations **participate,** but she also sees many families.
   - ☐ a. get involved
   - ☐ b. show up
   - ☐ c. plan
   - ☐ d. work hard

Making Connections

A Write each word from the list below in front of its definition as it is used in the selection.

debris **marine** **hazard** **estimate** **participate**

1. ______________________ relating to the sea
2. ______________________ to judge the amount of something
3. ______________________ the remains of something broken down
4. ______________________ to take part in
5. ______________________ something that is harmful

B Go back and read the paragraph in which each word appears, paying special attention to the sentence in which it is used. Then circle the word that has the same or almost the same meaning. Be prepared to support your choices.

1. **debris**	items	trash	materials	treasures
2. **marine**	water	animals	sea	land
3. **hazard**	busy	safety	obstacle	danger
4. **estimate**	calculate	confuse	subtract	predict
5. **participate**	work	partake	passive	avoid

C Complete each sentence with the correct vocabulary word.

debris **marine** **hazard** **estimate** **participate**

1. Tyler has played the trumpet for years and continues to ______________________ in the high school marching band.
2. The tornado left the streets scattered with ______________________.
3. I ______________________ that the drive will take three hours if we don't not make any stops.
4. Someone who studies the oceans' plant and animal life is a ______________________ biologist.
5. The icy, snow-covered roads are a ______________________ to motorists.

Personal Words Follow-up

Use a dictionary to find the definitions for the personal words you chose at the beginning of this lesson. If a word has more than one meaning, look for the meaning that defines the word as it is used in the selection. Then write the words and their dictionary definitions in the Personal Words pages at the back of the book. How close did you come to figuring out their meanings for yourself?

22 Word Study

A submarine travels under the water, and that is just what the parts of its name mean. The prefix *sub-* means "under," and the root *marine* means "sea." As an adjective, the English word *marine* means "of the sea." A marine-life aquarium is an aquarium for sea creatures. A related word is *marina.* A marina is a dock or harbor where boats can tie up and where supplies are available for small boats. A *mariner* is a sailor.

When submarines go below the water, we say that they submerge. The root *merge* means "to plunge or dive." So *submerge* naturally means "to dive under." Today we use the word *merge* to mean "to combine," or "to cause to be swallowed up or absorbed." It is often used when referring to the buying of one company by another, often larger company. One of the earliest meanings of *merge,* when it came into the English language, was "to drown." It's easy to see the connection between drowning and the words *dive* or *plunge.* To subtract, as you know, means to take away. The root *tract* means "draw." The Latin word *subtractus,* from which we got *subtract,* means "to draw from beneath," or "to withdraw."

Since *scribe* means "write," then a subscriber is someone who takes out a subscription by signing an agreement. *Scribe* also means "to approve or agree." If you *subscribe* to someone's opinion on a subject, you agree with him or her.

Word Part	Meaning	English Word
sub-	under	submarine
marine	of the sea	marina
merge	to plunge; to dive	submerge
tract	to remove by drawing back	subtract
scribe	to write; to approve; to agree	subscribe

Finding Meanings

Write each word or word part beside its meaning.

sub- **marine** **submerge** **scribe** **subscribe**

1. show agreement or approval ____________________
2. under ____________________
3. to dive under ____________________
4. of the sea ____________________
5. write ____________________

True or False

Write T if a statement is true or F if it is false.

__________ 1. The vessels known as submarines can travel on the surface of the water only.

__________ 2. If you agree with someone on an issue, you submerge to their point of view.

__________ 3. *Scribe* is another word for dive.

__________ 4. A mariner is a person who specializes in navigating over land.

__________ 5. To subscribe to a magazine is to sign up to have the magazine delivered to your home.

Choose an Answer

Put an **X** in front of the answer choice you think is correct.

1. A person who works as a crew member on a submarine is known as a
   - ☐ a. private.
   - ☐ b. submariner.
   - ☐ c. subscriber.

2. If you take 5 away from 8 you are
   - ☐ a. merging.
   - ☐ b. submerging.
   - ☐ c. subtracting.

3. A being that is less than human is known as a
   - ☐ a. superhuman.
   - ☐ b. extrahuman.
   - ☐ c. subhuman.

4. One who signs a form agreeing to have a newspaper delivered is a
   - ☐ a. subscriber.
   - ☐ b. scribe.
   - ☐ c. submerger.

5. If you are swimming without any kind of scuba gear, and you submerge, you had better
   - ☐ a. float on your back.
   - ☐ b. swim fast.
   - ☐ c. hold your breath.

23 Light Pollution

When our grandparents were children, the **splendor** of a dark night sky filled with stars and wrapped with the silky ribbon of the Milky Way was as close as the back door. The majesty of the night sky was visible from just about any backyard anywhere in the city or country.

That's not true anymore. A giant dome of light looms over every city in North America every night. Only the brightest stars and planets punch through the glow. Anyone who lives in or near a large city today sees just a few dozen stars instead of thousands. The lights of modern civilization have beaten back the stars. Most of us see the stars properly only when we are far away from a city.

I'm not suggesting that we don't need lighting at night. But the outdoor lighting we live with—streetlights, parking lot **illumination,** and so-called security lighting—is based largely on the **principle** that "more is better." This is the decade of environmental awareness, but all around us at night is light pollution. You can see light pollution everywhere once you are aware of it.

Have you ever been kept awake by streetlights shining in your bedroom window? There is no **logical** reason for that. Streetlights should illuminate just the street and sidewalk, not your home.

Most streetlights pump up to 30 percent of their light sideways, where they illuminate nothing but the eyes of distant drivers or the air above our heads. If cities installed better-designed streetlights that eliminated the wasted light shining off-target, they could use lower-wattage lamps. This type of lamp is called a full-cutoff fixture. It eliminates the waste and reduces glare for drivers but still lights the roadway.

Light pollution is an environmental issue whose time has come. Most outdoor lights waste energy by not properly targeting the light they **emit.** Correctly shielded lights require less electricity to do the job because they direct all the light where it is needed. If we don't start doing something about light pollution soon, we will lose the natural beauty of what little dark sky remains in areas reasonably close to where most people live.

Personal Words

Choose two words from the selection that are unfamiliar to you or whose meanings you are not completely sure of. (Do not choose words that appear in boldfaced type.) Write the words on the lines provided. Beside each word write what you think it means, based on how it was used in the selection.

1. ______________________ : ____

____

2. ______________________ : ____

____

Using Context

For each vocabulary word, put an **X** in the box beside its correct meaning. Try to figure out what the word means from the way it is used in the selection.

1. splendor
   - ☐ a. largeness
   - ☐ b. greatness
   - ☐ c. magic
   - ☐ d. color

2. illumination
   - ☐ a. magnification
   - ☐ b. filled with color
   - ☐ c. lamps
   - ☐ d. lighting

3. principle
   - ☐ a. belief
   - ☐ b. fact
   - ☐ c. saying
   - ☐ d. statement

4. logical
   - ☐ a. correct
   - ☐ b. incorrect
   - ☐ c. important
   - ☐ d. sensible

5. emit
   - ☐ a, create
   - ☐ b. bring
   - ☐ c. give off
   - ☐ d. take away

Making Connections

A For each vocabulary word, choose a synonym and an antonym from the following list. Write the synonyms and antonyms on the lines provided.

belief	**brightness**	**falsehood**	**magnificence**	**reasonable**
retain	**dullness**	**darkness**	**irrational**	**discharge**

	Synonym	**Antonym**
1. **splendor**	________________	________________
2. **illumination**	________________	________________
3. **principle**	________________	________________
4. **logical**	________________	________________
5. **emit**	________________	________________

B Complete the following analogies by inserting one of the five vocabulary words in the blank at the end of each one. Remember that in an analogy the last two words or phrases must be related to each other in the same way that the first two are related.

splendor **illumination** **principle** **logical** **emit**

1. idea : concept : : law : ____________________
2. automobile : exhaust : : streetlight : ____________________
3. intelligent : : smart : : sound : ____________________
4. construct : build : : eject : ____________________
5. stress : ease : : insignificance : ____________________

C On the line in front of each sentence, write the vocabulary word that has the same meaning as the underlined word or words.

splendor **illumination** **principle** **logical** **emits**

1. ____________________ The lighting up of the new ball field was great for the players but made area neighbors angry.
2. ____________________ There are few people who do not think it is reasonable to always wear your seatbelt when driving.
3. ____________________ At noon the sun gives off its most powerful rays, which is why sunscreen should be worn.
4. ____________________ As many times as Oscar looked through the telescope, the brilliance of the night sky always amazed him.
5. ____________________ "Do unto others as you would like them to do unto you" is a basic truth children should be taught at a young age.

Personal Words Follow-up

Use a dictionary to find the definitions for the personal words you chose at the beginning of this lesson. If a word has more than one meaning, look for the meaning that defines the word as it is used in the selection. Then write the words and their dictionary definitions in the Personal Words pages at the back of the book. How close did you come to figuring out their meanings for yourself?

24 Word Study

The worb part *ob-* has several different meanings. It can mean "toward," "to," or "against." In the word *object, ob-* has the latter meaning. To object is to express an opinion against an idea or action. As introduced in lesson 16, the root *ject* comes from the Latin *jacere,* meaning "to throw." In the word *objective, ob-* means "toward." An objective is a goal—something to move toward.

Another word that contains the root *ject* is *interject.* Since *inter-* means "between" or "among," to *interject* means "to throw between or into other things." If a conversation between people is *interrupted,* it is stopped or broken up. The interruption may be to *interject* a comment. *International* means "between nations." The *intersection* of two roads is the place where they cross or *intersect.*

Inter- is a prefix that has to do with position, direction, or time. *Intra-,* another prefix that has a similar purpose, means "within." You may have played on an *intramural* sports team. *Intramural* means "limited to participants within the bounds of an institution, such as a school." An intravenous injection is an injection made "within a vein."

Word Part	Meaning	English Word
ob-	toward; to; against	object
ject	to throw	object, injection
inter-	between; among	interject
intra-	within	intramural

Finding Meanings

Write each word or word part beside its meaning.

inter- **ob-** **intra-** **international** **object**

1. between nations ________________
2. to express disproval ________________
3. within ________________
4. between; among ________________
5. toward; to; against ________________

True or False

Write T if a statement is true or F if it is false.

_________ 1. A doctor uses a needle to interject medicine.

_________ 2. The intersection would be safer if stoplights were placed on each street.

_________ 3. The teacher objected to the student's rudeness.

_________ 4. An oblong box has six unequal sides.

_________ 5. When the boy interrupted, the conversation stopped.

Choose an Answer

Put an **X** in front of the answer choice you think is correct.

1. Because he strongly disagreed, he stood up and yelled, "I
   - ☐ a. oblige!"
   - ☐ b. overrule!"
   - ☐ c. object!"

2. The highway between Illinois and Wisconsin is an
   - ☐ a. intracity.
   - ☐ b. interstate.
   - ☐ c. international.

3. Medicine that must reach the bloodstream quickly is taken
   - ☐ a. intravenously.
   - ☐ b. objectively.
   - ☐ c. interrelated.

4. A meeting between two people about a job is called an
   - ☐ a. interjection.
   - ☐ b. interruption
   - ☐ c. interview.

5. If the basketball team you play on plays other teams from your school, your team is
   - ☐ a. interplay.
   - ☐ b. intrastate.
   - ☐ c. intramural.

21-24 Review and Extension

Multiple Meanings

Some of the vocabulary words you studied in lessons 21 and 23 have more than one meaning. Complete each sentence in this exercise with a vocabulary word from the list below. In these sentences, the words have different meanings than they had in the selection you read. If you are unsure of the various meanings of a word, look it up in the glossary.

estimated **emit** **hazard** **participate** **logical**

1. He was in severe pain but he did not ________________ a sound.
2. It is more ________________ to walk home over the bridge than to try crossing the busy street.
3. Mark's ________________ time for finishing the marathon was three hours, fifteen minutes.
4. In order to ________________ in the study, the candidates could not eat for 24 hours.
5. Sharp knives present a ________________ for young children.

Word Parts Review

Complete each sentence so that it makes sense and shows the meaning of the boldfaced vocabulary word.

1. The townspeople **objected** to the new traffic light because ________________

   ____
2. Because the ship **submerged** quickly, the sailors on deck ________________

   ____
3. The large, well-kept **marina** attracted many ________________

   ____
4. Even though the highway had signs, it was difficult to **merge** because ________________

   ____

5. "Mom," asked Edward, "could I please **subscribe** ______________________________

____

6. The captain shouted over the desert wind, "Step lively, people, our **objective** __________

____

7. It was easy to **subtract** small numbers, but it was not easy ____________________

____

8. The announcement over the loudspeaker **interrupted** the classes' ________________

____

9. Jakes's **intramural** volleyball team won only two games because _________________

____

10. Lisa's dream was to become a **mariner** because ______________________________

____

Synonym Study

Following are synonym studies for two vocabulary words you studied in lessons 21 and 23. Use either the vocabulary words or their synonyms to complete the sentences in this exercise. Refer to the synonym studies as you decide which choice carries the best meaning for the specific context of each sentence.

estimate **guess**

Estimate and *guess* both mean "to form a judgment of something." Estimate, however, is used when the value, size, or cost of something is considered before the judgment is made. *He estimated the height of the mountain.* Guess means to form an opinion without complete knowledge. *Without a clock she could only guess what time it was.*

1. Cindy managed to ____________________ the answer to the test question.

2. We were able to ____________________ her age based on the ages of her children.

debris **garbage**

Debris and garbage are both the remains of something. Debris refers to things broken down or destroyed. *After the earthquake debris filled the streets.* Garbage suggests that waste materials have been thrown away. *When the party was over, they picked up all the garbage.*

3. It was quite clear that the food and plates left in the park were ____________________
4. After the car accident, ____________________ was scattered all over the road.
5. Frieda cleaned up the ____________________ in the kitchen before her mother got home.

Word Forms

The words listed below are other forms of the vocabulary words you worked with in lessons 21 and 23. Fill in the blank in each sentence with the appropriate word. If you are unsure of the meaning of a word, look it up in the glossary.

estimation	**marina**	**illuminate**
logically	**participation**	**splendid**

1. It was easy to see why cleaning up the park required everyone's ____________________
2. During the 4th of July holiday, the ____________________ was filled with boats.
3. Her ____________________ was that the trip would take a total of 17 hours.
4. "The entire cast's performance was ____________________!" the newspaper critic declared.
5. The overhead lighting did more than ____________________ the hallways; it made the apartment building safer.
6. After ____________________ considering all his options, Steve decided to quit his job.

Using Your Vocabulary

This word-search puzzle contains 15 vocabulary words from lessons 17–24. They are printed horizontally, vertically, diagonally, backward, and upside down. Begin by writing the vocabulary words on a separate sheet of paper. Then find the words in the puzzle, circling them as you locate them.

1. half circle
2. guess
3. aim or goal
4. danger or source of harm
5. of the sea
6. carry from one place to another
7. sink below the surface
8. push forward
9. root meaning "to write"
10. many colors
11. relations between nations
12. sound thinking
13. great brightness
14. cause to happen
15. get involved with others

z	k	f	r	i	b	m	w	e	t	a	p	i	c	i	t	r	a	p	j	o	u	d	s	x	v	u
n	h	g	r	t	u	k	c	e	r	s	r	l	p	b	c	m	a	k	x	g	i	f	p	q	u	f
c	u	s	t	a	l	b	j	t	e	d	o	s	s	c	w	l	p	d	v	a	s	l	k	t	i	s
w	e	n	e	m	o	e	i	o	a	s	m	f	j	k	n	x	v	e	n	t	o	p	f	g	n	b
z	v	j	i	m	g	q	i	h	m	o	p	t	c	j	g	u	j	n	w	g	h	i	f	j	t	n
a	f	h	r	h	i	l	b	o	y	e	t	g	u	k	e	t	t	i	d	a	o	t	g	j	e	l
w	g	r	h	f	c	c	j	k	t	b	k	m	c	f	n	u	t	r	z	t	u	i	o	k	r	p
f	g	i	b	n	e	t	i	r	j	t	q	j	i	f	l	b	e	a	s	b	j	i	l	p	n	s
d	j	t	v	f	j	u	r	r	b	k	u	l	y	d	g	n	r	m	t	u	h	k	o	y	a	f
s	f	h	i	t	j	k	o	r	c	y	n	i	o	y	n	d	u	r	g	j	y	i	y	q	t	v
u	x	b	n	m	d	h	k	r	e	l	h	q	r	y	i	i	h	t	f	j	u	g	k	o	i	b
b	o	o	m	k	h	f	o	f	j	y	e	r	d	v	n	c	r	f	e	f	j	k	j	h	o	c
m	b	x	z	w	r	d	w	b	g	h	j	t	j	k	y	a	i	r	g	t	g	p	p	i	n	v
e	m	e	w	y	n	k	i	g	b	v	v	s	f	t	n	t	o	w	m	h	a	l	l	c	a	g
r	d	x	h	e	r	y	j	t	t	q	c	g	u	s	i	v	i	b	r	d	j	m	l	t	l	d
g	c	m	l	o	p	g	f	q	v	b	c	i	p	b	r	m	i	g	j	r	k	d	i	d	r	s
e	t	p	x	b	e	b	i	r	c	s	s	o	d	k	n	r	j	i	p	e	w	q	n	t	t	i
b	s	n	j	u	t	e	x	p	q	h	r	s	i	k	r	g	j	o	t	r	c	d	n	y	s	a
a	s	d	f	g	h	j	k	l	q	t	w	e	z	p	t	y	u	i	o	p	z	t	x	c	v	e
m	n	b	v	c	x	z	a	s	d	f	g	h	x	r	p	o	i	u	y	t	r	e	i	w	r	w
g	f	d	s	a	j	k	l	t	d	e	r	o	l	o	c	i	t	l	u	m	t	y	u	v	e	w
d	f	b	g	j	t	j	k	i	m	e	f	w	h	p	g	k	t	d	b	k	o	u	p	h	e	r
c	f	t	j	k	l	t	m	f	v	n	c	x	n	e	l	g	b	v	c	y	j	i	l	d	p	h
s	s	v	n	r	m	t	p	j	k	l	r	h	u	l	p	k	h	t	t	d	b	j	h	x	n	f

25 Fresco Painting

Fresco painting is a technique in which the artist paints on a plastered wall while the plaster is still damp. Fresco artists decorate both inside and outside walls. Fresco painting is especially well **suited** to decorating large walls in churches, government buildings, and palaces.

A wall must be carefully plastered before an artist paints a fresco on it. Usually, several layers of plaster are applied. The first layers are somewhat coarse. The final layer, called the *intonaco,* is smooth and bright white. The artist may plaster the wall, but most artists employ plasterers to do this work. The artist or plasterer does not apply the intonaco over the entire wall at once. Instead, the amount of intonaco that is applied is just enough for one day's painting.

A fresco painter applies paint to the wall while the plaster is still damp. The painter uses colors made of dry pigment that is mixed, in most cases, only with water. The plaster dries and hardens in about eight hours. The drying and hardening process seals the colors onto the wall.

The artist stops painting when the plaster is almost dry because the pigments—mixed only with water—will not stick to dry plaster. At the next working session, the artist gives the final coat of plaster to the area next to the part of the fresco that was finished **previously.** The artist then **resumes** painting, keeping the seam, or *join,* between the two sections as neat as possible.

Fresco plaster bleaches many colors. Therefore, not all pigments used in other painting techniques can be used in fresco painting. Fresco painters get the best **results** from soft, not too brilliant colors. These artists frequently use grays, rust tones, and tans.

Fresco painting reached its greatest popularity from the 1200s through the 1500s. Italy was the center of fresco painting during that period. During the 1900s, Mexican artists **revived** fresco painting. Mexican artists decorated many public buildings with large frescoes that show scenes from Mexican history.

Personal Words

Choose two words from the selection that are unfamiliar to you or whose meanings you are not completely sure of. (Do not choose words that appear in boldfaced type.) Write the words on the lines provided. Beside each word write what you think it means, based on how it was used in the selection.

1. ______________________ : ____

____

2. ______________________ : ____

____

Using Context

Put an **X** in the box beside each correct answer. For clues to the meanings of the words, reread the parts of the passage in which they appear.

1. The fact that fresco painting is **suited** to decorating large walls means that the method
   - ☐ a. can be used only on large walls.
   - ☐ b. was invented for decorating large walls.
   - ☐ c. is appropriate for large surfaces.
   - ☐ d. is inappropriate for large surfaces.

2. The part that was finished **previously** was completed
   - ☐ a. earlier.
   - ☐ b. very quickly.
   - ☐ c. professionally.
   - ☐ d. later.

3. To **resume** painting means to
   - ☐ a. enjoy it.
   - ☐ b. forget about it.
   - ☐ c. finish it.
   - ☐ d. begin again after an interruption.

4. To get the best **results** from certain colors means to
   - ☐ a. enjoy using them the most.
   - ☐ b. get the best effects from them.
   - ☐ c. get the most for your money.
   - ☐ d. get the best adhesion from them.

5. The Mexican artists who **revived** fresco painting
   - ☐ a. disliked the method.
   - ☐ b. discovered old fresco paintings.
   - ☐ c. argued against its usefulness.
   - ☐ d. brought it into use again.

Making Connections

A Write each word from the list on the line in front of its definition.

suited **previously** **resume** **result** **revive**

1. ____________________ outcome; good or useful effect
2. ____________________ appropriate or fitting
3. ____________________ bring back into use or fashion
4. ____________________ begin again; go on from where one left off
5. ____________________ before; earlier

B Write each vocabulary word on the line in front of the appropriate synonym and antonym.

suited **previously** **resume** **result** **revive**

	Synonym	Antonym
1. ______________	before	after
2. ______________	renew	end
3. ______________	restart	quit
4. ______________	effect	cause
5. ______________	fitted	mismatched

C Complete each sentence with the correct vocabulary word.

suited **previously** **resume** **result** **revive**

1. School is scheduled to ______________ on January 3, after a two-week vacation.
2. Orchids that grow in the tropics are not ______________ to the cold climate of the north.
3. The twins' decision not to dress alike brought the desired ______________. People could finally tell them apart.
4. Elaine hoped to ______________ her sister's interest in dance by taking her to the ballet.
5. Because she had visited the museum ______________ Kathy was able to lead her cousin to the most interesting exhibits.

Personal Words Follow-up

Use a dictionary to find the definitions for the personal words you chose at the beginning of this lesson. If a word has more than one meaning, look for the meaning that defines the word as it is used in the selection. Then write the words and their dictionary definitions in the Personal Words pages at the back of the book. How close did you come to figuring out their meanings for yourself?

26 Word Study

The prefix *mega-* means “large.” A megalopolis is an extremely large city or a region that embraces many large cities with no rural stretches between them. *Mega-* can also mean “one million.” A megavolt is one million volts, and a megameter is one million meters.

One of the meanings of *metro* is “mother.” The Greek root *polis* means “city.” A *metropolis,* is a “mother city” or a major city. A metropolis is the center of a metropolitan area that includes the city and nearby suburbs and small towns.

Another root that means “large” or “great” is the Latin *magni.* When *magni* is combined with the suffix *-fy,* which means “to make or to cause to be,” it forms the word *magnify,* which means “to make greater.” *Magnitude* is made up of the root *magni* and *tude,* which means “the state or quality of.” *Magnitude* can also mean “size as in the sentence *The weather bureau was not sure what the magnitude of the storm woul be.* Or it can refer to the quality or importance of something as in the phrase *the magnitude of family values.*

Word Part	Meaning	English Word
mega-	large; one million	megalopolis, meg
polis	city	metropolis, metr itan
metro	mother	metropolis
magni	large; great	magnify
-fy	to make; to cause to be	
tude	state; quality of	magnitude

Finding Meanings

Write each word or word part beside its meaning.

metro **polis** **mega-** **magnify** **magni**

1. large; great ______________
2. to make greater ______________
3. city ______________
4. large; one million ______________
5. mother ______________

True or False

Write T if a statement is true or F it is false.

_______ 1. An urban region containing several large cities is a megalopolis.

_______ 2. A megavolt has two million volts.

_______ 3. If the magnitude of a job is overwhelming, it probably requires a lot of work.

_______ 4. Looking through a magnifying glass will make something appear smaller.

_______ 5. New York is a metropolis.

Answering Questions

1. If magnitude refers to largeness, what would exactitude refer to? _______

____

2. If you magnify your friends' faults, how might they react? _______

____

3. When the mayor of a small town refers to the town as "a growing metropolis," is he exaggerating or being humble? _______

____

4. Why would someone take a megavitamin pill? _______

____

5. How would you describe the magnitude of a mouse? _______

____

27 Oil Painting

Oil paint is made by mixing powdered pigments with a binder of vegetable oil. Linseed oil is the most common binder. Artists buy oil paints in the form of thick pastes packaged in tubes. If an artist wants the paint to be more **fluid,** he or she adds a painting medium made of linseed oil, varnish, and turpentine.

Certain features of oil paint make it popular with artists who want to show the natural appearance of the world around them. Oil paint dries slowly. Therefore, the artist has time to blend the strokes into each other carefully and to adjust the color mixtures to **reproduce** natural appearances. Oil paint—even when applied thickly—does not crack as easily as water paint or egg tempera. As a result, the painter can apply oil paint in varying thicknesses to produce a wide **range** of textures.

Each artist develops his or her own method of working with oil paint. Many use some **variation** of the following steps. First, the artist puts on a wooden palette a small dab of each color he or she **intends** to use in the painting. The artist can mix colors on the palette to produce new tones. A small cup clipped to the corner of the palette holds paint thinner.

Usually, before beginning to paint, the artist draws the important outlines on the canvas or panel with charcoal or a pencil. Some artists attempt to achieve their final effects immediately. They paint all the colors and details in a few sessions or even at a single session. This method is called *direct painting* or *alla prima.* If an artist can use this method without making any corrections, the picture will appear lively, natural, and unified.

Personal Words

Choose two words from the selection that are unfamiliar to you or whose meanings you are not completely sure of. (Do not choose words that appear in boldfaced type.) Write the words on the lines provided. Beside each word write what you think it means, based on how it was used in the selection.

1. ____________________ : ____

____

2. ____________________ : ____

____

Using Context

Put an **X** in the box beside each correct answer. For clues to the meanings of the words, reread the parts of the passage in which they appear.

1. Many use some **variation** of the following steps.
   - ☐ a. hint or clue
   - ☐ b. color
   - ☐ c. slightly changed form
   - ☐ d. number

2. Therefore, the artist has time to blend the strokes into each other carefully and to adjust the color mixtures to **reproduce** natural appearances.
   - ☐ a. contrast with
   - ☐ b. give birth to
   - ☐ c. make exactly like
   - ☐ d. eliminate

3. As a result, the painter can apply oil paint in varying thicknesses to produce a wide **range** of textures.
   - ☐ a. variety
   - ☐ b. roughness
   - ☐ c. strip
   - ☐ d. palette

4. If an artist wants the paint to be more **fluid,** he or she adds a painting medium made of linseed oil, varnish, and turpentine.
   - ☐ a. thick
   - ☐ b. liquid
   - ☐ c. brightly colored
   - ☐ d. easy to remove

5. First, the artist puts on a wooden palette a small dab of each color he or she **intends** to use in the painting.
   - ☐ a. dislikes
   - ☐ b. plans
   - ☐ c. hopes
   - ☐ d. asks

Making Connections

A Complete the following analogies by inserting one of the five vocabulary words in the blank at the end of each one. Remember that in an analogy the last two words or phrases must be related to each other in the same way that the first two are related.

fluid **reproduce** **range** **variation** **intend**

1. ask : request : : plan : ______________________
2. excitement : calm : : sameness : ______________________
3. full : inflate : : same : ______________________
4. rock : solid : : water : ______________________
5. hint : clue : : choice : ______________________

B On the line next to each word or phrase, write the vocabulary word that is related to it. The related word may be a synonym, an antonym, or a definition for the vocabulary word.

fluid **reproduce** **range** **variation** **intend**

1. sameness ____________________
2. mean ____________________
3. copy exactly ____________________
4. solid ____________________
5. difference ____________________
6. flowing ____________________
7. spectrum ____________________
8. imitate ____________________
9. have as a purpose ____________________
10. a series between limits ____________________

C Complete each sentence with the correct vocabulary word.

fluid **reproduce** **range** **variation** **intend**

1. Adding bananas to the chocolate cake was a ____________________ on the usual recipe.
2. The Scanlons had dozens of photographs from their trip to New York, but the camera could not ____________________ the feeling of the trip.
3. On roller skates, Victor's movements were ____________________ and graceful.
4. Mr. Phelps did not ____________________ to prevent his students from continuing their discussion of the way in which grades are determined.
5. Miguel felt overwhelmed by the ____________________ of different bicycles he had to choose from.

Personal Words Follow-up

Use a dictionary to find the definitions for the personal words you chose at the beginning of this lesson. If a word has more than one meaning, look for the meaning that defines the word as it is used in the selection. Then write the words and their dictionary definitions in the Personal Words pages at the back of the book.

28 Word Study

The word part *auto-* means "self." *Auto-* can be combined with other word parts to form words such as *autobiography, autograph,* and *automobile.* Knowing that *auto-* means "self" will help you figure out the meanings of many other words. For example, *mobile* means "capable of moving," so an automobile is a self-powered machine that moves. This accounts for the name of what may be the most popular vehicle in history.

The root *graph* means "to write." An autograph is a person's own signature. *Photo* means "relating to or producing light." Light is necessary to photograph, or produce an image of an object. *Photograph* means literally "to write with light. *Phone* means "sound," and a phonograph is a device that writes with sound.

Another word part is *tele-,* which means "at a distance" or "far." We have all spoken on the telephone to people far away. *Tele-* can also be combined with *graph* to form *telegraph,* a system of sending messages over a distance. A telephoto lens is one that enlarges the image of a distant object.

Word Part	**Meaning**	**English Word**
auto-	self	autobiography
graph	to write	autograph, telegraph
photo	relating to or producing light	photograph, telephoto
phone	sound	phonograph, telephone
tele-	at a distance; far	telephone, telegraph

Finding Meanings

Write each word or word part beside its meaning.

tele- **photo** **autograph** **graph** **phone**

1. a person's own signature ________________
2. far ________________
3. sound ________________
4. light ________________
5. to write ________________

True or False

Write T if a statement is true or F if it is false.

_______ 1. The root meaning of *photograph* is "sound writing."

_______ 2. A mobile home stays in one place.

_______ 3. People can listen to a variety of music on a phonograph.

_______ 4. Autograph collectors collect signatures of famous people.

_______ 5. If we know vision means "to see," then a television is something that receives images and sounds that are nearby.

Choose an Answer

Put an **X** in front of the answer choice you think is correct.

1. When you do something without even thinking, your action is said to be
   - ☐ a. autographed.
   - ☐ b. automatic.
   - ☐ c. photographic.

2. Something that moves under its own power is
   - ☐ a. motive.
   - ☐ b. graphed.
   - ☐ c. mobile.

3. A story of a person's own life written by herself is an
   - ☐ a. autobiography.
   - ☐ b. biography
   - ☐ c. autograph.

4. To make the distant sailboat appear closer, the photographer used a
   - ☐ a. telegraph.
   - ☐ b. telephoto lens.
   - ☐ c. photographic lens.

5. Someone who looks very good in pictures is said to be
   - ☐ a. autograph.
   - ☐ b. photogenic.
   - ☐ c. phonographic.

25-28 Review and Extension

Multiple Meanings

Some of the vocabulary words you studied in lessons 25 and 27 have more than one meaning. Complete each sentence in this exercise with a vocabulary word from the list below. In these sentences, the words have different meanings than they had in the selection you read. If you are unsure of the various meanings of a word, look it up in the glossary.

suit **revive** **reproduce** **range**

1. Rescue workers were able to ____________________ the elderly man who had passed out from the heat.
2. Rabbits are known to ____________________ in extremely large numbers.
3. Gordon discovered that stamp collecting was the perfect hobby to ____________________ his unathletic nature.
4. The New York designers tried hard to ____________________ the miniskirt fashion of the sixties.
5. The eight Warner children ____________________ in age from five to seventeen.
6. The ____________________ brought against Mr. Rizzo's company for hiring illegal immigrants was bad for business.
7. Rebecca had taught herself to ____________________ the calls of a number of kinds of birds.
8. When babies are born, their ____________________ of vision is very limited.

Word Parts Review

Complete each sentence so that it makes sense and shows the meaning of the boldfaced vocabulary word.

1. Driving down the highway, Don knew that he was in a **megalopolis** from the fact that

   ____

2. The actor spent much of his time after performances signing **autographs** because

   ____

3. No one had guessed the **magnitude** of Wendell's wealth until his will was read and it was discovered that ____

____

4. Without the **telephoto** lens they would be able to see ________________________

____

5. The scientist needed a microscope to **magnify** the object before she could __________

____

6. Sandra's mother wondered if the **telephone** was such a great invention after her daughter

____

7. After the bombing stopped, the lieutenant hurried to **telegraph** ________________

____

8. The **automobile** driver avoided the crash by ____________________________

____

9. Fernando found a family **photograph** from the 1950s that ______________________

____

10. The **mobile** military unit ____

____

Synonym Study

Following are synonym studies for three vocabulary words you studied in lessons 25 and 27. Use either the vocabulary words or their synonyms to complete the sentences in this exercise. Refer to the synonym studies as you decide which choice carries the best meaning for the specific context of each sentence.

imitate **reproduce**

Imitate and *reproduce* both have to do with copying. To imitate is to try to copy someone's action, sound, or style. *Jack liked to imitate his father's walk.* To reproduce is to make an identical copy of a thing. *The artist could not reproduce the colors of the leaves exactly.*

1. Clair tried to ________________________ the lovely flower garden she had seen at her uncle's house in her own yard.

2. When learning to speak, babies ________________________ the sounds they hear from the people around them.

revive **refresh**

The words *revive* and *refresh* both concern bringing a person or thing back to a lively state. To revive is to bring back to life something that has fallen into disuse or ill health over time. *The play was revived 20 years after its original production.* To refresh is to bring new vibrancy, energy, or strength to something that has faded or weakened. *Nancy planned to refresh her room with a new coat of paint.*

3. There was an attempt on the part of some of the townspeople to

________________________ the tradition of an annual community picnic.

4. Having driven 200 miles without a stop, Jim and Henry decided to

________________________ themselves with a hearty lunch.

plan **intend**

Plan and *intend* are verbs that describe different kinds of thinking about an action before the action is taken. To plan is to decide beforehand how something is to be done. The entire family helped plan the trip to Washington. To intend means to have a particular purpose in mind. Claire intended to save all her money for new clothes.

5. Leah did not ________________________ to have anything to do with her sister's scheme to skip school on Friday.

6. The drama club scheduled a meeting for anyone interested in helping to

________________________ the next production.

Word Forms

The words listed below are other forms of the vocabulary words you worked with in lessons 25 and 27. Fill in the blank in each sentence with the appropriate word. If you are unsure of the meaning of a word, look it up in the glossary.

intends intention intended intending

variation various variety vary

fluid fluidity

revived reviving revival

suited suit suitable

results result resulted resulting

range ranged ranging

Joe was not in a good mood. He stood in the garage staring at the ______ (1) draining from the '92 Chevy he was working on. He thought about one hundred things, ______ (2) from fast cars to elegant dates with his girlfriend to a trip to California. All of them had one thing in common: they required lots of money. Joe ______ (3) to earn that money somehow.

Unfortunately, the only job really ______ (4) for him was simple car maintenance. "Nothing wrong with being a grease monkey," he thought, "but it won't ______ (5) in the really big bucks I want."

The paycheck Joe received for 40 hours of pumping gas and changing oil was not large. At the end of every month, he was just about broke. And that sad condition always brought a ______ (6) of his desire for ready cash. Joe yearned for the day when he could afford the ______ (7) of experiences that for now he could only dream of.

Using Your Vocabulary

Use vocabulary words from lessons 21–28 to complete the crossword puzzle.

ACROSS
1. a huge city
4. reasonable
6. earlier
7. discharge
10. system for sending coded messages
12. a different form of something
13. great size
14. prefix meaning "distance"

DOWN
2. a person's own signature
3. a lighting up
5. appropriate or fitting
6. a picture from a camera
8. a system for sending speech over distances
9. limited to players from the same school
11. to vary within set limits

29 What Is a Skeleton?

The skeleton is an important part of a body. It forms a strong **framework,** supporting the body's weight and giving it its own particular shape. It protects the soft, **essential** organs such as the brain, lungs, and heart, on which we depend for life. The skeleton also helps us to move. Our bones work with muscles to move our bodies, so that, for example, we can walk to a shelf, pick up a book, and turn a page.

It is an amazing thought that everyone you meet is a walking collection of bones. Adults have roughly 200 bones inside them. Bones vary greatly in size and shape. Some are long and straight with knobby ends, others are curved, and a few are small and round like pebbles. This varied collection fits together to form the skeleton, a sturdy yet **flexible** structure. Each part of the skeleton has its own special task. For example, the skull is a strongbox designed to protect the brain; the bones in the arm and hand form a piece of machinery that can move with both power and skill.

Every move we make depends on our bones and muscles working together. When we want to move, our brain sends a signal to our muscles, telling them to **contract.** When muscles contract, they pull on tough cords called tendons, which then move the bones. Without bones, muscles would have nothing to pull on; without muscles, bones couldn't move.

A skeleton can move only at places, called joints, where two bones meet. There are two main kinds of joints. A ball-and-socket joint **swivels** around in almost any direction. These joints are found in the shoulders and hips. A hinge joint allows a bone to bend or straighten. Hinge joints are found in fingers, elbows, and knees.

Our joints move countless times every day. Without some form of protection, the bones would slip out of place or grind together and lose their shape. To avoid this, bones are bound at the joints by straps called ligaments, which keep the bones firmly in place. The whole joint is coated in an oily liquid, which helps it to move smoothly and easily, over and over again.

Personal Words

Choose two words from the selection that are unfamiliar to you or whose meanings you are not completely sure of. (Do not choose words that appear in boldfaced type.) Write the words on the lines provided. Beside each word write what you think it means, based on how it was used in the selection.

1. ______________________ : ____

____

2. ______________________ : ____

____

Using Context

Put an **X** in the box beside the best definition for each boldfaced word. For clues to the meanings of words, reread the parts of the passage in which they appear.

1. It forms a strong **framework,** supporting the body's weight and giving it its own particular shape.
   - ☐ a. outline
   - ☐ b. building
   - ☐ c. bones
   - ☐ d. structure

2. The skeleton also protects the soft, **essential** organs such as the brain, lungs, and heart, on which we depend for life.
   - ☐ a. necessary
   - ☐ b. secondary
   - ☐ c. not important
   - ☐ d. helpful

3. A ball-and-socket joint **swivels** around in almost any direction.
   - ☐ a. moves from side to side
   - ☐ b. shakes
   - ☐ c. turns freely
   - ☐ d. bends

4. When we want to move, our brain sends signals to our muscles, telling them to **contract.**
   - ☐ a. an agreement
   - ☐ b. draw together
   - ☐ c. push out
   - ☐ d. flex

5. This varied collection fits together to form the skeleton, a sturdy yet **flexible** structure.
   - ☐ a. not bendable
   - ☐ b. flimsy
   - ☐ c. movable
   - ☐ d. soft

Making Connections

A Write each word from the list below in front of its definition as it is used in the selection.

framework **essential** **flexible** **contract** **swivels**

1. ______________________ draw together
2. ______________________ very important
3. ______________________ turns freely
4. ______________________ a structure that gives support to something
5. ______________________ able to bend without breaking

B Complete the following analogies by inserting one of the five vocabulary words in the blank at the end of each one. Remember that in an analogy the last two words or phrases must be related to each other in the same way that the first two are related.

framework **essential** **flexible** **contract** **swivels**

1. depressing : joyful : : unnecessary : ______________________
2. plastic : solid : : rubber : ______________________
3. joint : bends : : muscle : ______________________
4. pull : tug : : twist : ______________________
5. paper : outline : : building : ______________________

C On the line in front of each sentence, write the vocabulary word that has the same meaning as the underlined word or words.

framework **essential** **flexible** **contract** **swiveled**

1. ______________________ Louis knew it was extremely important to pass his final exams if he wanted to graduate on time.
2. ______________________ After heat was applied to the plastic, it was capable of being moved.
3. ______________________ Elizabeth turned the piano stool in the direction of her audience.
4. ______________________ Because the structure of the school was well-built, only the windows were damaged in the storm.
5. ______________________ We saw the frightened worm make itself smaller when the child tried to pick it up.

Personal Words Follow-up

Use a dictionary to find the definitions for the personal words you chose at the beginning of this lesson. If a word has more than one meaning, look for the meaning that defines the word as it is used in the selection. Then write the words and their dictionary definitions in the Personal Words pages at the back of the book. How close did you come to figuring out their meanings for yourself?

30 Word Study

A word part added to the end of a word or root is called a *suffix.* Often, adding a suffix changes both a word's part of speech and its meaning. The suffixes *-able* and *-ible* mean "able to," "likely," or "capable of being." Adding the suffix *-able,* to the verb *enjoy,* meaning "to receive pleasure from" forms the adjective *enjoyable,* meaning "capable of giving pleasure." The Latin root *edere* means "to eat." Something that is *edible* is "able to be eaten" or "fit to eat."

The suffixes *-ant* and *-ent* can mean "acting in a particular manner" or "one who does an action." The verb *observe,* meaning "to see" or "to notice," can be combined with the suffix *-ant* to form the adjective *observant,* which means "seeing" or "noticing." A person who studies is a *student,* and a person who serves others is a *servant.*

The verb *inhabit* means "to live or reside in." When *inhabit* is combined with *-ant,* the word becomes a noun, *inhabitant,* meaning "a person who lives in a certain place." When *-able* is added, the adjective *inhabitable,* meaning "able to be lived in," is formed.

Word Part	Meaning	English Word
-able, -ible	able to; likely; capable of	enjoyable, edible
-ant, -ent	doing; being; acting in a particular manner	observant, student servant
inhabit	to live in	inhabitant, inhabitable

Finding Meanings

Write each word or word part beside its meaning.

-ent **enjoyable** **inhabitant** **observant** **-ible**

1. doing; being ____________________
2. one who lives in a place ____________________
3. able to; likely ____________________
4. capable of giving enjoyment ____________________
5. alert ____________________

True or False

Write T if a statement is true or F if it is false.

__________ 1. Legible handwriting is hard to read.

__________ 2. If a sandcastle is destructible, it is not likely to fall apart.

__________ 3. An observant student might not notice a message on the classroom door.

__________ 4. A town's inhabitants might be expected to vote in the mayoral election.

__________ 5. The occupant of an apartment can probably park her car in the building's garage.

Choose an Answer

Put an **X** in front of the answer choice you think is correct.

1. Something that bends easily without breaking is
   - ☐ a. inhabitable.
   - ☐ b. flexing.
   - ☐ c. flexible.

2. When he used a telescope, the planets and stars were
   - ☐ a. enjoyable.
   - ☐ b. observable.
   - ☐ c. inhabitable.

3. If you oppose, or compete against, another player, you are that person's
   - ☐ a. opposite.
   - ☐ b. opponent.
   - ☐ c. competent.

4. A car with a roof that folds back is called a
   - ☐ a. changeable.
   - ☐ b. converter.
   - ☐ c. convertible.

5. When construction is finished, a new house is
   - ☐ a. comfortable.
   - ☐ b. inhabitable.
   - ☐ c. inhabitant.

31 The Human Skeleton

Like fish, birds, and reptiles, and like other mammals, humans have bony skeletons inside their bodies. The bottom half of the skeleton—from the hips to the feet—allows us to walk **upright.** The top half includes the skull, arms, and hands, which contain our equipment for seeing, hearing, smelling, touching, and tasting.

The two halves of a skeleton are linked together by the backbone, which is also called the spine. Most animals walk on four legs, and so their spines are **horizontal.** But humans walk on two legs, and so the spine is upright, supporting us as we stand. And yet the spine is not straight like a tent pole. Looked at from the side, it forms a curving S-shape. This shape helps to strengthen the spine so that it can **absorb** jolts when we walk or run. It also helps to balance the top half of the body over the hips and legs.

The human backbone is built of 33 pillar-shaped bones called vertebrae, some of which are **fused** together. Vertebrae at the top of the spine are small, but they get larger and heavier toward the base, where they carry more of the body's weight. Inside each vertebra is a hollow arch. The arches of all these vertebrae line up to form a long, bony tunnel called the spinal or vertebral column. The tunnel contains and protects the spinal cord, a vital nerve that runs down the spine, carrying messages from the brain to the body and back again.

The vertebrae are linked together at joints. The joint between each pair of vertebrae can only move a little bit, but along the whole vertebral column these small movements combine to give us enough flexibility to arch backwards, twist around, or bend forward and touch our toes.

To most of us, bones are the dry, white sticks we see in museums. Yet in a living body, bones are nothing like that. Bone is moist, living tissue. Just like our skin, it contains blood vessels, nerves, and a **mass** of busy cells. Bone also contains a substance called calcium, which makes it rigid and hard. This is combined with long, stretchy fibers called collagen. The combination of calcium phosphate and collagen makes bone tough but flexible, like all the best building materials.

Personal Words

Choose two words from the selection that are unfamiliar to you or whose meanings you are not completely sure of. (Do not choose words that appear in boldfaced type.) Write the words on the lines provided. Beside each word write what you think it means, based on how it was used in the selection.

1. ______________________ : ____

____

2. ______________________ : ____

____

Using Context

Put an **X** in the box beside each correct answer. For clues to the meanings of the words, reread the parts of the passage in which they appear.

1. If someone walks **upright,** the person is walking
   - ☐ a. hunched over.
   - ☐ b. straight up.
   - ☐ c. upstairs.
   - ☐ d. correctly.

2. An animal's spine is **horizontal,** which tells us it is
   - ☐ a. long and wide.
   - ☐ b. straight.
   - ☐ c. vertical to the ground.
   - ☐ d. parallel to the ground.

3. The spine will **absorb** the jolts from walking or running, which means that the energy of the jolts is
   - ☐ a. taken in.
   - ☐ b. used up.
   - ☐ c. pushed out.
   - ☐ d. pulled away.

4. If vertebrae are **fused** together, they are
   - ☐ a. shaped the same.
   - ☐ b. in a row.
   - ☐ c. separated.
   - ☐ d. joined together.

5. From the sentence in which **mass** appears, you can tell that it means a
   - ☐ a. small amount.
   - ☐ b. section.
   - ☐ c. quantity of matter.
   - ☐ d. piece of an object.

Making Connections

A Write each word from the list below in front of its definition as it is used in the selection.

upright **horizontal** **absorb** **fused** **mass**

1. ______________________ in a vertical position
2. ______________________ a quantity of matter
3. ______________________ blended together
4. ______________________ parallel to the horizon
5. ______________________ take in

B Write each vocabulary word on the line in front of the appropriate synonym and antonym.

upright **horizontal** **absorb** **fused** **mass**

	Synonym	Antonym
1. ______________	hold	release
2. ______________	erect	flat
3. ______________	quantity	one
4. ______________	together	apart
5. ______________	level	slanted

C Complete each sentence with the correct vocabulary word.

upright **horizontal** **absorb** **fused** **mass**

1. To keep the chemicals from spilling, the scientist kept them ______________ in a test tube.
2. At exactly nine o'clock, the guard opened the doors and a ______________ of people filled the shopping mall.
3. For a bad back, some people recommend lying on a hard ______________ surface for several hours.
4. The two classes ______________ into one to work on a community service project.
5. As Martin jumps into bed, the bedsprings ______________ his weight.

Personal Words Follow-up

Use a dictionary to find the definitions for the personal words you chose at the beginning of this lesson. If a word has more than one meaning, look for the meaning that defines the word as it is used in the selection. Then write the words and their dictionary definitions in the Personal Words pages at the back of the book. How close did you come to figuring out their meanings for yourself?

32 Word Study

The prefix *epi-* means "upon," "near," or "over." The root *demos* means "people." In the word *epidemic, epi-* means "over." So epidemic means "spreading over the people." A rapidly spreading contagious illness would be an epidemic. A popular type of clothing that everyone is wearing might be called a fashion epidemic. The word *epidermis* looks similar but means something very different from *epidemic.* Dermis means "skin," so the epidermis is the layer of skin that is over all the other layers. A *dermatologist* is a doctor who practices *dermatology*—the study and treatment of skin diseases.

Hypo- means "under," "beneath," or "below." *Hypodermic* means "lying beneath the skin," or "injected beneath the skin," as with a hypodermic needle. Someone who has extremely low blood pressure has *hypotension.*

Another prefix that has a meaning similar to *epi-* is *hyper-*. *Hyper-* means "over," "above," or "beyond." A *hyperactive* child is one that is overly active. Someone who is *hypercritical* is overly critical.

Word Part	Meaning	English Word
epi-	upon; near; over	epidemic, epidermis
demos	people	epidemic
dermis	skin	epidermis, dermatology, hypodermic, hypnotized
hypo-	under; beneath; below	hypodermic, hypotension
hyper-	over; above; beyond	hyperactive, hypercritical

Finding Meanings

Write each word or word part on the left beside its meaning on the right.

hypo- **demos** **epi-** **hyperactive** **epidemic**

1. spreading over people ____________________
2. on; over; around; next to ____________________
3. people ____________________
4. under; beneath; below ____________________
5. overly active ____________________

True or False

Write T if a statement is true or F if it is false.

_________ 1. An epidemic is a sickness that affects only the outer layer of skin.

_________ 2. Since *epi-* means "upon" and *graph* means "to write," an epigraph is an inscription engraved on something.

_________ 3. The doctor injected the hypodermic needle over the skin.

_________ 4. The bubonic plague that swept across Europe in the 14th century was a deadly epidermis.

_________ 5. Hyperactive people might have trouble sitting through a long movie.

Choose an Answer

Put an **X** in front of the answer choice you think is correct.

1. Since *demos* means people, it stands to reason that an epidemic is a disease that sweeps across a wide area and affects many
   - ☐ a. people.
   - ☐ b. doctors.
   - ☐ c. dermatologists.

2. An actor or an actress would probably not want to appear before an audience that was
   - ☐ a. hypercritical.
   - ☐ b. hypocritical.
   - ☐ c. hypodermic.

3. If dermatology is the study and care of skin diseases, one who specializes in this branch of medicine is called a
   - ☐ a. epidermis.
   - ☐ b. democracy.
   - ☐ c. dermatologist.

4. A person who has high blood pressure suffers from
   - ☐ a. dermatology.
   - ☐ b. hypodermic.
   - ☐ c. hypertension.

5. A video game craze that spreads rapidly, becoming a widespread fad, could be called an
   - ☐ a. epicycle.
   - ☐ b. epidemic.
   - ☐ c. epicenter.

29-32 Review and Extension

Multiple Meanings

Some of the vocabulary words you studied in lessons 29 and 31 have more than one meaning. Read each word listed below and its definitions. Complete each sentence that follows with the correct vocabulary word.

flexible

a. (adj.) able to bend without breaking
b. (adj.) able to adjust easily to change

contract

a. (v.) to draw together to make shorter or make smaller
b. (v.) to get or acquire
c. (v.) to establish by agreement

absorb

a. (v.) to take in or soak up
b. (v.) to take up all the attention of
c. (v.) to take in and make part of itself

1. A sponge can ______________________ water very quickly.
2. To ______________________ the flu, one must usually be around others who are sick.
3. The rubber mat was so ______________________ it could be rolled up easily.
4. Your muscles ______________________ when you do sit-ups.
5. The carpeted room will ______________________ most of the sounds that come and go in their house.
6. Jon's schedule was ______________________ enough that he could leave early and catch the show.
7. In order to ______________________, the worm uses all its muscles and forms a ball.
8. Terri tries to ______________________ as many new words as she can each day to learn Spanish.
9. Being very ______________________ helped the gymnast win first prize on the uneven bars.

10. Even with music and talking all around him, Sam can ____________________ everything he reads.

Word Parts Review

Complete each sentence so that it makes sense and shows the meaning of the boldfaced vocabulary word.

1. The newspapers began calling the large number of flu cases an **epidemic** when ________

   ____

2. The zoo was **enjoyable** for Randy, since he ____________________

   ____

3. When Marilyn found out that the entire gingerbread house was **edible,** she __________

   ____

4. The **dermatology** textbook was filled with pictures of ____________________

   ____

5. In her **hypercritical** way, Tania said " ____________________

   ____

6. A **hypodermic** needle was injected ____________________

   ____

7. Since the first sign of disease was a bluish discoloration of the **epidermis,** Karl got worried when he noticed that ____________________

   ____

8. Only an **inhabitant** of the building would know ____________________

   ____

9. On her report card it said she was bright and **observant,** which meant __________

   ____

10. To keep the ordinarily **hyperactive** children calm, the teacher __________

    ____

Synonym Study

Following are synonym studies for three vocabulary words you studied in lessons 29 and 31. Use either the vocabulary words or their synonyms to complete the sentences in this exercise. Refer to the synonym studies as you decide which choice best fits the context of each sentence.

swivel **rotate**

Swivel and *rotate* both mean "to turn." Swivel suggests that a link allows an attached part to turn freely. *To see the computer and work at his desk, he had to swivel his chair one way, then the other.* Rotate means "to turn around on a straight line or axis" or "to alternate." *The earth rotates from west to east.*

1. The guards will ________________________ every six hours.
2. Your arm is able to ________________________ because of a ball-and-socket joint.
3. Maria had to ________________________ the globe to see North America.

essential **urgent**

Essential and *immediate* are both adjectives that refer to something necessary or important. Essential implies that something is very important and cannot be ignored. *It is essential that we arrive early for the surprise party.* Urgent suggests that something needs immediate attention or action, or an earnest pleading. *The director of the hospital made an urgent call for funds.*

4. The fire department had an ________________________ call that could not wait.
5. To pass the class, it was ________________________ to read all the material.
6. Your heart is one of your most ________________________ organs.

absorb **receive**

Absorb and *receive* both mean "to take something in." Absorb suggests soaking something up but also taking up all the attention of someone. *She was very absorbed in the movie despite the subtitles.* Receive implies something is taken into one's possession or experienced. *He received the news about the accident only hours after it happened.*

7. On her birthday, she will ________________________ more cards than anyone you know.

8. The teacher knew Martin would ________________________ a shock when he saw the grade on his paper.

9. The paper towels could not ________________________ all the juice from the broken bottle.

Word Forms

Each sentence below requires you to use two vocabulary words you studied in lessons 29 and 31. Fill in the blanks in each sentence with the appropriate words. If you are unsure of the meaning of a word, look it up in the glossary.

essentially/horizontal **absorbed/contracted** **fusion/framework**

swiveling/upright **masses/flexibility**

1. Rather than ________________________ back and forth on a chair, Simon decided to stand ________________________ to follow the parade.

2. The ________________________ of the two metals created a ________________________ for the building that was stronger and more resistant to the elements.

3. The apartment building's walls usually ________________________ sound, but William was ________________________ under the sheets trying to ignore the party next door.

4. When ________________________ of snow were left behind after the storm, ________________________ and cooperation were required from everyone in town.

5. ________________________ the only way the bridge could be supported was to place many ________________________ beams in the middle.

Using Your Vocabulary

Use vocabulary words introduced in lessons 25–32 to solve this word puzzle. For each definition or synonym, think of a vocabulary word that has the same meaning. Write the word in the puzzle space beside its definition. The number of lines in each answer space and the letter that is given provide clues to the word. Notice that the circled letters form the title of a selection in these lessons. Write the title on the line provided.

1. the root meaning "at a distance" ○ _ _ _
2. straight up _ _ _ _ _ ○ _
3. structure _ _ _ _ ○ _ _ _ _
4. parallel to the ground ○ _ _ _ _ _ _ _ _ _
5. blend together _ ○ _ _
6. root meaning "skin" _ _ _ ○ _ _
7. a body of matter _ ○ _ _
8. necessary _ _ _ _ ○ _ _ _ _
9. turn freely ○ _ _ _ _ _

(k)

10. a widespread occurrence _ _ _ _ ○ _ _ _
11. easily bendable _ ○ _ _ _ _ _ _
12. the outer layer of skin ○ _ _ _ _ _ _ _ _
13. enlarges the image of a distant object _ _ _ _ _ _ _ ○ _
14. capable of giving pleasure _ _ _ ○ _ _ _ _ _
15. quick to notice _ _ _ _ _ _ _ ○ _

Title: ______________________________

Personal Words

Word	Definition

Word	Definition

Word	Definition

Word	Definition

Word	Definition

Glossary

Pronunciation Key

Symbol	Example	Symbol	Example
a	p**a**n	o͞o	m**oo**d
ā	m**a**ke	o͝o	t**oo**k
âr	d**are**	u	c**u**t
ä	f**a**ther	ûr	p**ur**ple
e	g**e**t	yo͞o	m**u**te
ē	s**ee**m	t͟h	**th**en
i	p**i**t	th	**th**in
ī	**i**ce	hw	**wh**at
îr	p**ier**	zh	u**s**ual
o	c**o**t	ə	**a**bout
ō	g**o**		list**e**n
ô	**aw**ful		penc**i**l
oi	s**oi**l		comm**o**n
ou	m**ou**th		camp**u**s

Stress marks: ′ (primary); ′(secondary) as in (vō·kab′yə·lər′ē)

A

absorb (əb·sôrb′) *v.* To take in; endure. **absorbed**

abundance (ə·bun′dəns) *n.* A quantity that is greater than enough; plenty.

abundant (ə·bun′dənt) *adj.* Plentiful; ample.

accent (ak′sent′) *v.* (1) To pronounce with particular stress or emphasis. (2) To stress or emphasize.

accentuate (ak·sen′choo·āt′) *v.* To increase the effect of; emphasize; stress.

acquire (ə·kwīr′) *v.* To come to possess; to obtain.

adapt (ə·dapt′) *v.* To make fit, often by making some changes.

adhere (ad·hîr′) *v.* (1) To stick fast; cling. (2) To support a person or an idea; to be loyal.

adherent (ad·hîr′ənt) *n.* A person who believes strongly in and sticks by a particular leader, cause, or idea.

adhesion (ad·hē′zhən) *n.* A thing that sticks; an attachment.

adhesive (ad·hē′siv) *n.* A substance that glues or pastes things together.

adjacent (ə·jā′sənt) *adj.* Next to; close by.

adopt (ə·dopt′) *v.* (1) To choose. (2) To formally accept or approve. (3) To choose to raise as one's own a child born to other people. **adopted**

adoption (ə·dop′shən) *n.* (1) The act of taking on by choice. (2) Formal acceptance; approval.

advent (ad′vent′) *n.* A coming into being; arrival.

affiliate (ə·fil′ē·āt′) *v.* (1) To join in close association; connect; unite. (2) *n.* Someone who is connected closely to an association. **affiliation**

affirm (ə·fûrm) *v.* (1) To give formal approval. (2) To state or declare firmly.

affix (ə·fiks′) *v.* To fasten or attach. **affixing**

affixed (ə·fikst′) *adj.* Fastened or attached.

attach (ə·tach′) *v.* To fasten by a link, tie, or bond.

attain (ə·tān′) *v.* (1) To arrive at, come to, or reach. (2) To obtain.

attainable (ə·tā′nə·bəl′) *adj.* (1) Reachable. (2) Possible to obtain.

attainment (ə·tān′mənt) *n.* The act of obtaining or reaching.

autobiography (ô′tə·bī·og′rə·fē) *n.* The story of a person's own life written by him or her self.

autograph (ô′tə·graf′) *n.* (1) A person's own signature. (2) Something written in a person's own handwriting.

automobile (ô′tə·mō·bēl′) *n.* A passenger vehicle usually having four wheels and driven by an engine powered by gasoline; car.

C

clever (klev′ər) *adj.* Mentally quick.

closet (kloz′it) *n.* A closed room for storing things. *v.* To shut off by oneself; to shut off in a private place.

collaborate (kə·lab′ə·rāt′) *v.* To work with another or others.

collate (kō′lāt) *v.* To arrange or gather in proper order.

collection (kə·lek′shən) *n.* (1) The act or process of collecting. (2) Something gathered together.

combine (kəm·bīn′) *v.* To bring two or more things together to form a new thing.

comfort (kum′fərt) *v.* To bring strength and hope; to offer cheer.

complete (kəm·plēt′) *adj.* Finished; whole; full.

compose (kəm·pōz′) *v.* To put together; to make up; to form.

composer (kəm·pō′zər) *n.* One who puts together, makes up, or forms something.

composition (kom′pə·zish′ən) *n.* (1) The way in which something is put together. (2) A thing that has been assembled, or put together, such as an essay or a musical piece.

conduct (kən·dukt′) *v.* (1) To lead or guide. (2) To carry out or perform. (3) To transmit, receive, or carry such things as electricity or heat. **conducted**

conductor (kən·duk′tər) *n.* (1) Someone who leads or guides. (2) Anything that transmits, receives, or carries energy.

configuration (kən·fig′yə·rā′shən) *n.* Form or shape resulting from the arrangement of parts.

configured (kən·fig′yərd) *v.* Designed; arranged; set up for a specific use.

confine (kən·fīn′) *v.* To keep within limits; restrict; shut in. **confined**

confirm (kən·fûrm′) *v.* (1) To prove to be true without mistakes; verify. (2) To approve. (3) To make firm or firmer; to strengthen.

congregate (kong′grə·gāt′) *v.* To come together in a crowd or mass; to assemble.

contract (kən·trakt′) *v.* To draw together; to make shorter or smaller.

convention (kən·ven′shən) *n.* (1) A gathering of people for a particular purpose. (2) Custom; the generally agreed upon behavior of a group of people.

convertible (kən·vûr′tə·bəl) *n.* (1) An automobile that has a top that can be folded back or removed. (2) Something that can be converted.

cult (kult) *n.* (1) A group showing great admiration for a person, thing, or idea. (2) Great admiration of a person, thing or idea.

D

debris (də·brē′) *n.* The remains of something broken down or destroyed; rubbish.

decade (dek′ād′) *n.* A period of ten years.

decode (dē·kōd′) *v.* To translate from, or take out of, code.

decompose (dē·kəm·pōz′) *v.* To rot; to separate into basic elements or ingredients.

deduct (di·dukt′) *v.* To take away; to remove.

deduction (di·duk′shən) *n.* (1) An amount taken away from the total earned. (2) An inference or conclusion arrived at through reasoning.

delineate (di·lin′ē·āt′) *v.* (1) To describe in detail. (2) To show or mark the outline of something. **delineating**

delineation (di·lin′ē·ā′shən) *n.* (1) The act of describing something in detail. (2) The act of pointing out or marking an outline. (3) A detailed description.

demigod (dem′ē·god′) *n.* An inferior or lesser god.

demitasse (dem′ē·tas′) *n.* (1) A small cup of black, usually strong coffee. (2) A small cup in which such coffee is commonly served.

demos Root meaning people.

derail (dē·rāl′) *v.* (1) To cause to go off the rails, or track. **derailed**

dermis Greek root meaning skin or covering.

dermatologist (dûr′mə·tol′ə·jist) *n.* A skin doctor.

dermatology (dûr′mə·tol′ə·jē) *n.* The branch of medicine that treats the skin.

destructible (di·struk′tə·bəl) *adj.* Capable of being destroyed; ruined completely.

detract (di·trakt′) *v.* To lessen in value, quality, or importance.

devote (di·vōt′) *v.* (1) To give all or most of one's attention to. (2) To give oneself over to a person or a cause.

devotion (di·vō′shən) *n.* Strong attachment or commitment shown by constant attention.

dictate (dik′tāt′) *v.* (1) To speak or read aloud to another person who writes down the spoken words. (2) To command or order.

diction (dik′shən) *n.* A person's manner of expressing ideas in words; a style of speaking or writing.

difficult (dif′i·kult′) *adj.* Hard to do or understand.

direct (di·rekt′) *adj.* Straightforward; frank.

disagree (dis′ə·grē′) *v.* To differ in opinion; to argue.

disagreement (dis′ə·grē′mənt) *n.* A difference of opinion; a quarrel; an argument.

disaster (di·zas′tər) *n.* An event causing much suffering or loss; sudden or great misfortune.

discipline (dis′ə·plin) *n.* (1) Orderly and obedient behavior. (2) Punishment used to teach a lesson. *v.* (1) To bring under control; to train. (2) To punish in order to correct or change behavior. **disciplined**

discontinue (dis′kən·tin′yo͞o) *v.* Stop; put an end to; cease. **discontinued**

discontinuing (dis′kən·tin′yo͞o·ing) *n.* Stopping; putting an end to; ceasing from.

disease (di·zēz′) *n.* A disturbance in the function of an organ or organism resulting from a specific cause or causes, such as an infection.

dislodge (dis·loj′) *v.* To move; to force out of a place or position.

disorient (dis·ôr′ē·ent′) *v.* To disturb the sense of direction or position of; to confuse. **disoriented**

distinction (di·stingk′shən) *n.* 1) Mark of difference or identification. (2) Excellence; honor.

distinctive (di·stingk′tiv) *adj.* Special; recognizably different.

E

edible (ēd′ə·bəl) *adj.* Capable of being eaten; fit to eat.

effect (i·fekt′) *n.* The result or consequence of an action. *v.* To bring about or cause to be.

effects (i·fekts′) *n.* Personal belongings or property.

ejection (i·jek′shən) *n.* The act of giving off, throwing out, or forcing out something; the condition of being ejected.

eliminate (i·lim′ə·nāt′) *v.* (1) To get rid of; to remove. (2) To leave out; to omit. (3) To expel from the body.

emit (i·mit′) *v.* To send forth; to give off; to discharge.

enjoy (en·joi′) *v.* To receive pleasure from.

enjoyable (en·joi′ə·bəl) *adj.* Giving or capable of giving pleasure.

epidemic (ep′i·dem′ik) *n.* (1) The widespread occurrence of a disease. (2) The outbreak or sudden spread of anything. *adj.* Affecting many people in a population.

epidermis (ep′i·dûr′mis) *n.* The outer layer of skin.

epigraph (ep′i·graf′) *n.* (1) An engraved inscription. (2) A quotation, often found at the beginning of a book, that hints at the book's theme.

essential (i·sen′shəl) *adj.* Very important or necessary.

estimate (es′tə·māt′) *v.* To form a judgment, as of the approximate value, quality, or size of something. **estimated**

estimation (es′tə·mā′shən) *n.* The act of estimating.

exactitude (eg·zak′tə·to͞od) *n.* The quality of being exact; accuracy; precision.

exceed (ek·sēd′) *v.* (1) To surpass or outdo; to go over the limit or record. (2) To go beyond the limit set by authority or custom. **exceeded**

excess (ek·ses′) *n.* An oversupply; more than enough.

exclude (eks·klo͞od′) *v.* To shut out or keep out.

exclusive (eks·klo͞o′siv) *adj.* (1) Not shared with others. (2) Shutting others out.

exhale (eks·hāl′) *v.* To breathe out.

expire (ek·spīr′) *v.* To come to an end; to die. **expired**

export (ek·spôrt′) *n.* A product sent out of a country. *v.* To send something out of a country.

exterior (ek·stîr′ē·ər) *n.* The outer surface or part; the outside. *adj.* Of; relating to; on the outside; outer; external.

extracurricular (ek′strə·kə·rik′yə·lər) *adj.* Not part of the regular course of study.

extraneous (ek·strā′nē·əs) *adj.* That which has little or nothing to do with the subject; irrelevant.

extraordinary (ek·strôr′də·ner′ē) *adj.* Beyond or above the usual or ordinary; very unusual.

extravagant (ek′strav′ə·gənt) *adj.* (1) Lavish or wasteful in the spending of money. (2) Beyond reasonable limits.

F

fix (fiks) *v.* (1) To attach or fasten firmly, to make stable. (2) To focus steadily. **fixed**

fixed (fikst) *adj.* Stationary; immovable; unchanging.

fixedly (fik′sid·lē) *adv.* Without moving.

flexible (flek′sə·bəl) *adj.* Able to bend without breaking; not stiff or rigid.

fluid (flo͞o′id) *n.* Liquid; gas; anything that flows. *adj.* Flowing; like a liquid or gas.

fluidity (flo͞o·id′ə·tē) *n.* Capability to flow.

fold (fōld) *v.* (1) To bring to an end; to go out of business. (2) To bend or double over itself. **folded, folding**

formalized (fôr′mə·līzd) *v.* Made official.

formally (fôr′mə·lē) *adv.* (1) Officially; with ceremony. (2) Precisely; according to set rules.

forte (fôr′tā′) *adv.* Musical term meaning in a loud or forceful manner.

framework (frām′wûrk′) *n.* a structure that gives shape or support to something.

fulfill (fo͝ol·fil′) *v.* To carry out or to live up to something, as a dream or promise.

fulfilled (fo͝ol·fild′) *adj.* Satisfied; content.

fulfillment (fo͝ol·fil′mənt) *n.* (1) The realization or accomplishment of something. (2) Contentment; satisfaction.

fuse (fyo͞oz) *v.* to blend thoroughly; to melt together. **fused**

G

garbage (gär′bij) *n.* Worthless matter; trash.

graduate (graj′o͞o·āt′) *v.* (1) To pass from one stage or level to a higher one. (2) To finish a course of study at a school. (3) To mark out in equal spaces for measuring. **graduated**

graduation (graj′o͞o·ā′shən) *n.* The ceremony marking the completion of a course of study.

H

hazard (haz′ərd) *n.* A source of danger or harm.

heliport (hel′ə·pôrt) *n.* A place where helicopters land and take off.

hemicycle (hem′i·sī′kəl) *n.* A curved or semicircular structure.

hemisphere (hem′i·sfîr′) *n.* One-half of the earth, as divided by the equator or the Greenwich and 180° meridians. (2) One-half of a sphere.

horizontal (hôr′i·zont′l) *adj.* Parallel to the horizon; level.

humble (hum′bəl) *adj.* Not grand, lofty or noble; modest and unassuming.

humility (hyo͞o·mil′ə·tē) *n.* A feeling of one's own insignificance; modesty.

hyperactive (hī′pər·ak′tiv) *adj.* Overly active.

hypercritical (hī′pər·krit′i·kəl) *adj.* Excessively critical.

hypertension (hī′pər·ten′shən) *n.* Abnormally high blood pressure.

hypodermic (hī′pə·dûr′mik) *adj.* (1) Lying beneath the skin. (2) Made to be injected under the skin.

hypotension (hī′pə·ten′shən) *n.* Abnormally low blood pressure.

I

illegal (il·lē′gəl) *adj.* Not legal.

illegible (i·lej′ə·bəl) *adj.* Incapable of being deciphered or read.

ill-humored (il′hyo͞o′mərd) *adj.* Irritable; grouchy; in a bad mood.

illiterate (i·lit′ər·it) *adj.* Being unable to read and write.

illogical (i·loj′i·kəl) *adj.* Not reasonable or correctly thought out; not following the rules of logic.

illuminate (i·lo͞o′mə·nāt′) *v.* To provide light.

illumination (i·lo͞o′mə·nā′shən) *n.* The state of being brightened with light; a lighting up.

imitate (im′i·tāt′) *v.* (1) To try to be like or act like someone else. (2) To follow a pattern or model. **imitating**

immobile (i·mō′bəl) *adj.* Incapable of being moved; not mobile.

implode (im·plōd′) *v.* (1) To burst inward. (2) To collapse inward as if from outside pressure.

import (im·pôrt′) *n.* An object that is brought in to one place from another place, usually a foreign country. *v.* To bring in, usually from a foreign place.

impossible (im·pos′ə·bəl) *adj.* Not capable of being or happening; not possible.

imprison (im·priz′ən) *v.* (1) To put or keep in prison. (2) To confine or restrain in any way. **imprisoned**

improperly (im·prop′ər·lē) *adv.* Not in accord with modesty, manners, or good taste.

incapable (in·kā′pə·bəl) *adj.* Lacking sufficient power, resources, or capability.

incorporate (in·kôr′pə·rāt) *v.* (1) To make something part of something else; to join or combine. (2) To form into a legal group of merchants, traders, or businesses. **incorporating, incorporation**

incorrect (in′kə·rekt′) *adj.* Not correct; not agreeing with fact or truth.

indicate (in′di·kāt) *v.* To point out; to show.

inhabit (in·hab′it) *v.* To live in; to reside in. **inhabited**

inhabitable (in·hab′it·ə·bəl) *adj.* Able to be lived in.

inhabitant (in·hab′i·tənt) *n.* A person who lives in a certain place.

injection (in·jek′shən) *n.* (1) The act of forcing a fluid into something for medical purposes. (2) The act of introducing a new element into something.

intelligent (in·tel′ə·jənt) *adj.* Having a high degree of mental ability.

intend (in·tend′) *v.* To have in mind as a particular purpose; to plan. **intended, intending**

intention (in·ten′shən) *n.* A purpose or plan one has in mind.

interject (in′tər·jekt′) *v.* To insert between or into other things.

interlude (in·tər·lo͞od′) *n.* (1) Something that fills the time between two other things. (2) A short piece of music, usually played between two longer pieces or between the acts of a play.

international (in′tər·nash′ə·nəl) *adj.* Having to do with two or more nations.

interrupt (in′tə·rupt′) *v.* To break in upon; to stop in the course of an action or speech. **interrupted**

intersect (in′tər·sekt′) *v.* (1) To divide by passing through or across. (2) To meet and cross at a point.

intersection (in′tər·sek′shən) *n.* A place where two or more things, such as roads, cross.

interstate (in′tər·stāt′) *adj.* Between or among two or more states.

interview (in′tər·vyo͞o′) *n.* A formal face-to-face meeting.

intramural (in′trə·myo͝or′əl) *adj.* Consisting of or limited to participants from the same school or organization.

intravenous (in′trə·vē′nəs) *adj.* Within or into a vein. *adv.* **intravenously**

invigorating (in·vig′ə·rā′ting) *adj.* Filling with life and energy.

issue (ish′o͞o) *n.* A debated point or matter of importance. *v.* To put into circulation; to deliver for use. **issued**

L

legible (lej′ə·bəl) *adj.* Capable of being read.

limit (lim′it) *n.* A boundary or restricting feature. *v.* To assign boundaries to something; to restrict.

lodge (loj) *v.* To get caught; to stay in one place. **lodged**

logic (loj′ik) *n.* Sound thinking; reasoning.

logical (loj′i·kəl) *adj.* Of, or relating to, sound thinking; reasonable.

M

magnify (mag′nə·fī′) *v.* To enlarge; to cause to look larger.

magnitude (mag′ni·to͞od′) *n.* (1) Great size. (2) Size regardless of largeness or smallness. (3) Importance.

maneuver (mə·no͞o′vər) *n.* Any skillful or clever move or plan. *v.* To make a change in position for a desired purpose. **maneuvered**

maneuverability (mə·no͞o′vər·ə·bil′i·tē) *n.* The quality of being able to be easily moved.

marina (mə·rē′nə) *n.* A dock or harbor where small boats can moor and where supplies and repair facilities are usually available.

marine (mə·rēn′) *adj.* Of or relating to the sea.

mariner (mar′ə·nər) *n.* A person who navigates or assists in navigating a ship; a sailor.

mass (mas) *n.* A body of matter holding or sticking together without a particular shape.

megalopolis (meg′ə·lop′ə·lis) *n.* A huge city, or a thickly populated area consisting of several large cities.

megameter (meg′ə·mē′tər) *n.* One million meters.

megavolt (meg′ə·vōlt′) *n.* One million volts.

mere (mîr) *adj.* No more than specified; only. *adv.* **merely**

merge (mûrj) *v.* (1) To combine into one. (2) To cause one thing (often a business) to be absorbed or swallowed up by another, so that the smaller thing loses its identity, simply becoming part of the larger.

metropolis (mə·trop′ə·lis) *n.* A large city, especially one that is an important center of commerce or culture.

metropolitan (met′rə·pol′i·tən) *adj.* Of or relating to a major city.

misbehave (mis′bi·hāv′) *v.* To behave badly.

miscalculate (mis·kal′kyə·lāt) *v.* To figure out incorrectly.

misconception (mis′kən·sep′shən) *n.* An incorrect understanding.

misinterpretation (mis′in·tûr′prə·tā′shən) *n.* An incorrect understanding of the facts at hand.

mobile (mō′bəl) *adj.* Capable of moving or of being moved from place to place.

multicolored (mul′ti·kul′ərd) *adj.* Of many or various colors.

multicultural (mul′ti·kul′chər·əl) *adj.* Of, relating to, or intended for several cultures.

multimillionaire (mul′ti·mil′yə·nâr′) *n.* A person who has several million dollars.

multiple (mul′tə·pəl) *adj.* Made up of or involving many or more than one. **multiples**

multiplication (mul′tə·pli·kā′shən) *n.* The process of adding a number to itself a certain number of times; increasing.

N

nonprofit (non·prof′it) *adj.* Not conducted or maintained for the purpose of making money over and above costs.

nonsense (non′sens′) *n.* Talk or action that does not make sense, that is foolish or silly.

O

obedient (ō·bē′dē·ənt) *adj.* Tending to follow the directions or commands of those in authority.

object (əb·jekt′) *v.* To express an opinion against an idea or action. **objected**

objective (əb·jek′tiv) *n.* A goal that seems capable of being reached.

oblong (ob′lông) *adj.* Longer in one dimension, as in a long loaf of bread, an egg shape, or a rectangle.

observable (əb·zûr′və·bəl) *adj.* That can be observed; noticeable.

observant (əb·zûr′vənt) *adj.* Quick to notice or perceive; alert.

observe (əb·zûrv′) *v.* To see or notice.

occupant (ok′yə·pənt) *n.* A person who occupies a place or position.

opponent (ə·pō′nənt) *n.* One who is against something.

orient (ôr′ē·ənt) *v.* (1) To get or fix the location or bearings of. 2) To adjust to a new situation.

origin (ôr′ə·jin) *n.* (1) The beginning, the starting point. (2) The thing from which anything comes.

originate (ə·rij′ə·nāt′) *v.* (1) To come into being; to begin. (2) To cause to be; to invent. **originated**

overcoat (ō′vər·kōt′) *n.* A heavy outer coat worn over clothing for added warmth.

overdress (ō′vər·dres′) *v.* (1) To dress too warmly. (2) To dress too well or elaborately for a social occasion. **overdressed**

overlook (ō′vər·lo͞ok′) *v.* To miss or omit because of neglect. **overlooked**

oversight (ō′vər·sīt′) *n.* A failure to notice or see something; the omission of something that should have been seen, done, or included.

overstate (ō′vər·stāt′) *v.* To express something too strongly; to exaggerate.

overwhelm (ō′vər·hwelm′) *v.* To overpower or upset someone by being too great, strong, heavy, or difficult.

P

participate (pär·tis′ə·pāt′) *v.* To take part or have a share with others, as in an activity. **participated** *n.* **participation**

pause (pôz) *n.* A temporary stop in action.

peculiar (pi·kyo͞ol′yər) *adj.* Characteristic of one thing or type of thing.

phonograph (fō′nə·graf′) *n.* A record player.

photogenic (fō′tə·jen′ik) *adj.* Attractive as a subject for photography.

photograph (fō′tə·graf′) *n.* A picture made with a camera. *v.* To take pictures with a camera.

plan (plan) *v.* To think out beforehand how something is to be done.

port (pôrt) *n.* A place where ships anchor or dock.

portable (pôr′tə·bəl) *adj.* (1) Capable of being carried. (2) Easily carried or moved. *n.* Something that is portable, such as a laptop computer.

porter (pôr′tər) *n.* A person who carries things for others.

postpone (pōst·pōn′) *v.* To put off to a later time.

postscript (pōst′skript′) *n.* A message or note added to a letter after the writer's signature; added material.

posttest (pōst′test′) *n.* A test given after completion of a program.

posture (pos′chər) *n.* (1) The position of the body; the manner of holding the body. (2) The condition, situation, or state of something.

precede (pri·sēd′) *v.* To go before in time or order.

precook (prē·ko͞ok′) *v.* To cook part way before finally cooking, or before reheating.

predict (pri·dikt′) *v.* To tell in advance that something is going to happen.

prediction (pri·dik′shən) *n.* (1) The act of predicting. (2) Something foretold or predicted; a prophecy.

prefix (prē·fiks′) *n.* A word part that is attached in front of a baseword or a root.

prejudge (prē·juj′) *v.* To judge beforehand or without knowing all the facts.

prejudice (prej′ə·dis) *n.* An opinion formed without taking the time and care to judge fairly; a judgment made before knowing all the facts.

prepay (prē·pā′) *v.* To pay for beforehand.

previous (prē′vē·əs) *adj.* Coming or made before; earlier. *adv.* **previously**

principle (prin′sə·pəl) *n.* a basic truth, law, belief, or doctrine.

procedure (prə·sē′jər) *n.* (1) A series of steps followed in a regular, definite order. (2) A way of accomplishing something.

proceed (prō·sēd′) *v.* (1) To move forward. (2) To carry on with an activity.

project (prə·jekt′) *v.* To throw; to force forward.

prompt (prompt) *v.* (1) To move to action. (2) To inspire. (3) To supply a performer or speaker with words he or she has forgotten. **prompted**

promptly (prompt′lē) *adv.* In a timely manner; on time.

propel (prə·pel′) *v.* To drive forward by a force that creates motion.

propeller (prə·pel′ər) *n.* A device consisting of a central hub and revolving blades that is attached to boats and aircraft to drive the vehicles forward.

protest (prō′test) *n.* An expression of disapproval or objection. (prə·test′) *v.* To express disapproval or objection.

R

range (rānj) *n.* The extent of variations within set limits. *v.* To vary within certain limits. **ranged, ranging**

recede (rē·sēd′) *v.* (1) To move back or away; to withdraw. (2) To grow less or smaller.

receive (ri·sēv′) *v.* To take or acquire; to get.

recess (rē′ses′) *n.* (1) A short intermission between periods of work or school. (2) A cavity in a wall that is set back, or in, from the rest of the wall. *v.* To suspend work or school for relaxation.

recluse (rek′lo͞os′) *n.* A person who chooses to live alone, apart from society.

redo (rē·do͞o′) *v.* To do again.

reduce (ri·do͞os′) *v.* (1) To make less or smaller; to decrease. (2) To change to another form. (3) To bring to a certain state or condition. **reduced**

reduction (ri·duk′shən) *n.* The act of lessening or making smaller.

refresh (ri·fresh′) *v.* To bring new strength or energy to something or someone. **refreshed**

reject (ri·jekt′) *v.* (1) To throw back. (2) To refuse to accept, consider, or submit to. **rejected**

remedy (rem′ə·dē) *n.* A means of relieving disease; a cure. *v.* To put right; to cure. **remedied**

renew (ri·no͞o′) *v.* (1) To restore something to freshness or vigor. (2) To restore something to its original state.

repair (ri·pâr′) *v.* To fix something that is broken.

repay (ri·pā′) *v.* To pay back.

reply (ri·plī′) *v.* To respond or answer.

report (ri·pôrt′) *n.* A written or spoken account of an event.

reporter (ri·pôr′tər) *n.* A person employed to gather and report news for a newspaper, magazine, or television.

reproduce (rē′prə·do͞os′) *v.* (1) To make an identical copy. (2) To produce offspring. **reproduced**

responsible (ri·spon′sə·bəl) *adj.* Having as a job, duty, or concern. (2) Faithful to duties; trustworthy; reliable.

restoration (res′tə·rā′shən) *n.* Renewal; repairing of damages or injuries done.

restore (ri·stôr′) *v.* To return something to its original condition. **restored**

result (ri·zult′) *n.* Something that occurs or is brought about because of an earlier action, process, or condition; an effect.

resume (ri·zo͞om′) *v.* To begin again; to go on from where one left off. **resumed**

revival (ri·vī′vəl) *n.* A bringing back to life, consciousness, or awareness.

revive (ri·vīv′) *v.* (1) To bring back into fashion or use. (2) To bring back or come back to life or consciousness. **revived, reviving**

rotate (rō′tāt′) *v.* (1) To turn or spin on an axis. (2) To proceed in sequence.

S

seasoned (sē′zənd) *adj.* Grown experienced over a period of time.

semiannual (sem′ē·an′yo͞o·əl) *adj.* Happening twice a year, especially at six-month intervals.

semicircle (sem′i·sûr′kəl) *n.* A half circle or something arranged in or resembling a half circle.

semimonthly (sem′ē·munth′lē) *adj.* Appearing or happening twice a month.

semiofficial (sem′ē·ə·fish′əl) *adj.* Having some degree of authority; partly official.

semiprecious (sem′ē·presh′əs) *adj.* Valuable but having less value than precious stones.

sensation (sen·sā′shən) *n.* (1) Something that causes a feeling. (2) A great interest.

sensational (sen·sā′shə·nəl) *adj.* Causing or meant to cause great interest.

servant (sûr′vənt) *n.* One hired to serve others.

shrewd (shro͞od) *adj.* Clever; of good judgment.

solve (sôlv) *v.* To find the answer to a puzzle or problem.

solvent (sôl′vənt) *n.* A substance that can dissolve other substances.

splendid (splen′did) *adj.* Outstanding; grand; magnificent.

splendor (splen′dər) *n.* (1) A great display, as of riches or beautiful objects; magnificence. (2) Great brightness; brilliance.

sprightly (sprīt′lē) *adj.* Having a lively, brisk quality.

stern (stûrn) *adj.* Severe; serious looking; harsh.

strenuous (stren′yo͞o·əs) *adj.* Requiring much energy and stamina.

student (sto͞od′nt) *n.* A person attending a school, college, or university to study something.

subhuman (sub′hyo͞o′mən) *adj.* (1)Below the human race. (2) Not fully human.

submarine (sub′mə·rēn′) *n.* A ship that can go underwater as well as on the surface. *adj.* Below the surface of the sea.

submariner (sub′mə·rē′ner) *n.* A member of the crew of a submarine.

submerge (səb·mûrj′) *v.* (1) To sink underwater. (2) To put something under water; to cover something with water.

submissive (səb·mis′iv) *n.* Yielding to the power or control of another; obedient.

subscribe (səb·scrīb′) *v.* (1) To promise to accept and pay for something. (2) To approve or agree. *n.* **subscriber**

subtract (səb·trakt′) *v.* (1) To take away or deduct from another number. (2) To perform the process of subtraction. **subtracting**

suffix (suf′iks′) *n.* A word part added to the end of a word that changes the word's meaning.

suit (so͞ot) *n.* A case in a court of law. *v.* (1) To make fit or appropriate. (2) To be appropriate for; to agree with.

suitable (so͞o′tə·bəl) *adj.* Right for the occasion; fitting or appropriate.

suited (so͞o′tid) *adj.* Appropriate; fitting.

sustain (sə·stān′) *v.* (1) To supply with food or other needed things; support. (2) To undergo or experience. **sustained**

sustenance (sus′tə·nəns) *n.* A means of supporting life; food and supplies.

swivel (swiv′əl) *v.* To turn or swing freely. **swiveled**

T

telegraph (tel′ə·graf′) *n.* The system, process, and equipment used for sending messages over a distance with coded electrical impulses.

telephone (tel′ə·fōn′) *n.* An electrical system for sending sound or speech over distances.

telephoto (tel′ə·fō′tō) *adj.* Being a camera lens system that gives a large image of a distant object. *n.* (1) A telephoto lens. (2) A photograph taken with a camera having a telephoto lens.

television (tel′ə·vizh′ən) *n.* A system of sending and receiving images and sounds by changing them into signals, which are turned back into picture and sound by a receiving set.

transatlantic (trans′ət·lan′tik) *adj.* Crossing the Atlantic Ocean.

transfer (trans·fûr′) *n.* The carrying of information or an object from one place to another. *v.* To carry or send something from one place to another.

transport (trans·pôrt′) *v.* To carry something from one place to another. **transported**

tribulation (trib′yə·lā′shən) *n.* Great trouble or distress.

troupe (tro͞op) *n.* A group or company of people, particularly performers.

try (trī) *v.* (1) To test; to push to the limit. (2) To attempt; to undertake. **tried**

trying (trī′ing) *adj.* Testing one's strength or patience to the limit.

U

uncivilized (un·siv′ə·līzd′) *adj.* (1) Not civilized; savage; wild. (2) Not following the social customs of society.

understudy (un′dər·stud′ē) *n.* A person trained to act as a substitute for a regular performer. *v.* To study another actor's part in order to substitute in an emergency.

upright (up′rīt′) *adj.* In a vertical position; straight up; erect.

urgent (ûr′jənt) *adj.* Needing immediate action; important.

V

variation (vâr′ē·ā′shən) *n.* A somewhat different form of something.

variety (və·rī′ə·tē) *n.* A number of different kinds of a group or thing.

various (vâr′ē·əs) *adj.* Of different kinds.

vary (vâr′ē) *v.* To change; to make different.

vigor (vig′ər) *n.* Healthy energy or power; active strength.

vigorous (vig′ər·əs) *adj.* Having power and energy.

Word and Word Part List

Vocabulary Drills, Middle